IMAGES
of America

ELMWOOD PARK

In 1939, Elmwood Park celebrated its silver anniversary. Although the country was still suffering from the effects of the Great Depression, the village had much to celebrate. The municipal building is decked out in patriotic red, white, and blue bunting. The celebration began at 2:00 p.m. on June 25 and lasted 10 days. (Courtesy of the Elmwood Park Library.)

ON THE COVER: A young boy and his passenger pedal across Grand Avenue in Elmwood Park as the village kicks off its 25th anniversary. A quarter of a century earlier, a visitor to the corner of Harlem and Grand Avenues would have been greeted with the tents of real estate agents and apple orchards. In the foreground, note the tracks of the Grand Avenue streetcar line, which terminated at Harlem Avenue. (Courtesy of the Elmwood Park Library.)

IMAGES
of America

ELMWOOD PARK

Kenneth J. Knack

ARCADIA
PUBLISHING

Published by Arcadia Publishing
Charleston, South Carolina

Library of Congress Control Number: 2013941156

For all general information, please contact Arcadia Publishing:
Telephone 843-853-2070
Fax 843-853-0044
E-mail sales@arcadiapublishing.com
For customer service and orders:
Toll-Free 1-888-313-2665

Visit us on the Internet at www.arcadiapublishing.com

To my wonderful wife, Diane—you continue to inspire me!

CONTENTS

ACKNOWLEDGMENTS

In my study of Elmwood Park's history, I have viewed anniversary books, articles, and newspaper clippings and have come to realize that this project would have been impossible without the help and support of the following people. Firstly, I wish to thank Frank Vesper, Edwin Emmerling, and Russ Parker, who took the time to compile most of the photographs and articles that provided the foundation of my research, including many of the images found on the following pages. I also would like to thank the photographers themselves for capturing the places and faces frozen in time.

My task was made much easier by the support of village president Peter Silvestri and his administration, as well as the Elmwood Park Library Board of Trustees: Gabe Caporale, Terri Sorrentino (president), Nancy Okal, Jonathan Zivojnovic, Orlando Vale, Marisa Santangelo, and Carmen P. Forte Jr. The library staff, including directors Shawn Schaeffer and Tiffany Verzani, Jason Stuhlmann, Dan Beringhele, and the others I met on my many visits to the local history room, were of immense help. The staff of Arcadia Publishing, specifically Amy Perryman, Kelsey Jones, Maggie Bullwinkel, and Tim Sumerel, also deserve thanks.

I would like to thank Bill Kucera, Sheila Severino, and Michael Warnock for contributing photographs.

Additionally, I would like to thank the following institutions and organizations for contributing photographs: the Elmwood Park Fire Department, including Chief Mike Ventura and firefighters Bill Kucera and David Zin; St. Celestine's Parish, including its pastor, Rev. Jeffrey S. Grob; as well as Barbara Kubiniec-Mares and Maria Malo; Franklin Park Public Library and Karen Gurski, local history librarian; and School District 401, including Nancy Lasselle, Laura Schulze, and Jim Jennings.

Others who provided stories, resources, or encouragement include my wife, Diane, my mother, Virginia, and my extended family. I also wish to thank Kim Parrilli, Rosemarie Biancalana, Dino Braglia, Deputy Police Chief Andrew Hock of the Village of Elmwood Park, village manager Paul Volpe, Anthony Biscaglio, Carl Nordlie, Video Ray, Mario Novelli, and the Facebook group "Elmwood Park, Memories of Places Gone Bye," from whom I learned a lot. I also want to thank all of those who sent photographs or suggestions, even if I did not use the material.

Unless otherwise indicated, photographs and images are from the Elmwood Park Library's history center. In the following pages, I will try to capture the essence of a community 100 years in the making. It is impossible to list all of the business, people, and events that have shaped the village, so I hope you will find my attempt at chronicling this history a noble one.

INTRODUCTION

As Elmwood Park's centennial approached, I thought it would be appropriate to gather images of the village spanning the past 100-plus years and incorporate them into a history. I moved into Elmwood Park in 2006, a relative newcomer, although I had a passing familiarity with the area. I had patronized the Mercury Theatre, eaten at Johnnie's and Russell's, and bought tires at the Sears Auto Center. I had even purchased a tree at Handy Andy. Every village has a story, and I knew that Elmwood Park deserved its rightful place among the Arcadia series of local history books.

The first residents were Native Americans, who occupied what is now the vicinity of Evans Field. The location was known as both a chipping station and a signal station, where they would make weapons and tools needed for daily life. After treaties were signed in which the Indians gave up the rights to their land to the US government, the territory was surveyed and sold at land auctions. Speculators purchased large tracts of land for next to nothing, then turned around and sold subdivisions of the land. When the initial land grab was completed, farmers settled into the area. The prairie soil was fertile, and they found that their crops and produce would grow easily. From the 1830s until the turn of the century, the area was mostly unincorporated and sparsely populated. The exception was the area north of the tracks, just west of Harlem Avenue. This little area was known as Orison from 1850 until 1905. Later, it was called Ellsworth.

In 1914, a group of residents decided to incorporate the area. The name they chose was Elmwood Park, a name that had been used for the train station around 1903. The incorporation set off several building booms. One of the first was led by John Mills & Sons, who had a development called Green Fields on the south end of town. A few years later, their Westwood development changed the village in a huge way. By the time the 25th anniversary occurred, the community was well established. The Great Depression brought growth to a standstill, but the postwar years would see another population spike. In 1920, the population was a mere 1,380; by 1961, it had surpassed the 20,000 mark.

Never really a manufacturing area, the community had more of a retail- and service-based economy. Grand Avenue was the main street of the village. Unfortunately, very few vintage buildings survive along that stretch. It seems that buildings were constructed only to be replaced a few years later. The other shopping areas are located along Harlem, North, and Belmont Avenues. In addition to the shopping, many restaurants, delis, and corner grocery stores flourished. Elmwood Park is first and foremost a residential community.

The growth of Elmwood Park coincided with the migration of Italian Americans from the old neighborhoods in Chicago. Many extended families moved to the village. In fact, when the village decided to adopt a sister city in 1997, it chose Frosinone, Italy. At that time, 34 percent of the village was of Italian decent.

It turns out that the village of Elmwood Park is slightly mislabeled. It was said at one time that Oak Park had many more elms and that Elmwood Park had many more oaks. When John Mills built Westwood, his men planted hundreds of elm trees. As the trees matured, they created a canopy over the village streets. Sadly, Dutch elm disease killed most of those elms. Some of them were replaced by ash trees as well as by maples, locusts, and other varieties.

The past 60 years can be divided into two relatively distinct periods. First are the Conti years. From 1953 to 1985, Elmer Conti served as village president. That period was what some would call an age of innocence. The town had all the modern conveniences that come with city living, yet there were still wild and open areas to explore, with cops chasing kids from Frankenstein Hill or Bums Tunnel. It was a slower time, when playing Little League baseball, bike riding, or visiting a playground could fill summer days and nights. It was an era when people could leave their doors unlocked. A sense of community prevailed, reaching its zenith in the golden jubilee in 1964. Those years were followed closely by the Silvestri era, which began in 1989.

During the Silvestri era, new challenges emerged. Among them were aging infrastructure and a change in demographics, as people continued to move farther west in search of larger and newer homes. The village has faced those challenges by modernizing facilities and acquiring sites to increase parkland. A new library was built on almost the same site as the very first library. The two most recent changes were the election of Angelo "Skip" Saviano as the first new village president since 1989, and the flood mitigation project of 2013.

A village is a collection of individuals, and I have made a valiant effort to include as many names, places, and facts as I can. This book, limited to 224 images, makes impossible a complete history, so I have attempted to capture the essence of the community. In the course of compiling this book, I inevitably came across contradictions. I have done my best to be as accurate and thorough as possible, and I humbly apologize for any errors or omissions. I hope the reader finds this to be an enjoyable trip down memory lane, or a good introduction to the village of Elmwood Park.

One

ORIGINS

The Pottawatomie tribe was the last in a long line of Native American peoples to inhabit this area. It has also been home to the Ottawa, Sacs, Foxes, Chippewa, and Miami tribes. The area of Evans Field in southwest Elmwood Park was once a very important site to many Indians. At the turn of the 20th century, an archaeologist named Kennicott identified several mounds in the area, near Russell's Barbecue. Centuries ago, what is now Lake Street was a major trail from Lake Michigan to the villages along the Des Plaines River, once called "la rivière Des Plaines" and also known as "Aux Plaines." The trail from the lake branched off, with one leg leading into what became Forest Park and the other toward the site at Evans Field.

After the treaty of Prairie du Chien was signed in July 1829, the Native Americans ceded their lands, with the exception of two large reservations for Chiefs Alexander Robinson and Claude La Framboise. The area was then surveyed and sold at land auctions. The area's 12 sections, comprising 1,280 acres, were owned by 11 men. Among the original landowners was Jean Baptiste Beaubien. He was married to Josette La Framboise, and he owned the land from Fullerton Avenue south to Armitage Avenue and from Seventy-sixth Avenue east to Harlem Avenue. Beaubien had been one of the very first settlers in the Chicago area. Those original buyers purchased the land at $1.25–$1.50 an acre. Many of the original owners were speculators who never settled here and would sell their lands a few years later for $1,500–$5,000 an acre.

B. Rhodes, a surveyor of English descent, built a home just south of Fullerton Avenue at about 7307 West in 1847. He later sold it to Fryer Marwood, who granted the railroad rights to cross his land. In 1873, the line was built, nearly running through his front yard. The tracks also crossed Whiskey Point Road, now known as Grand Avenue. A development known as Orison sprouted up at this juncture.

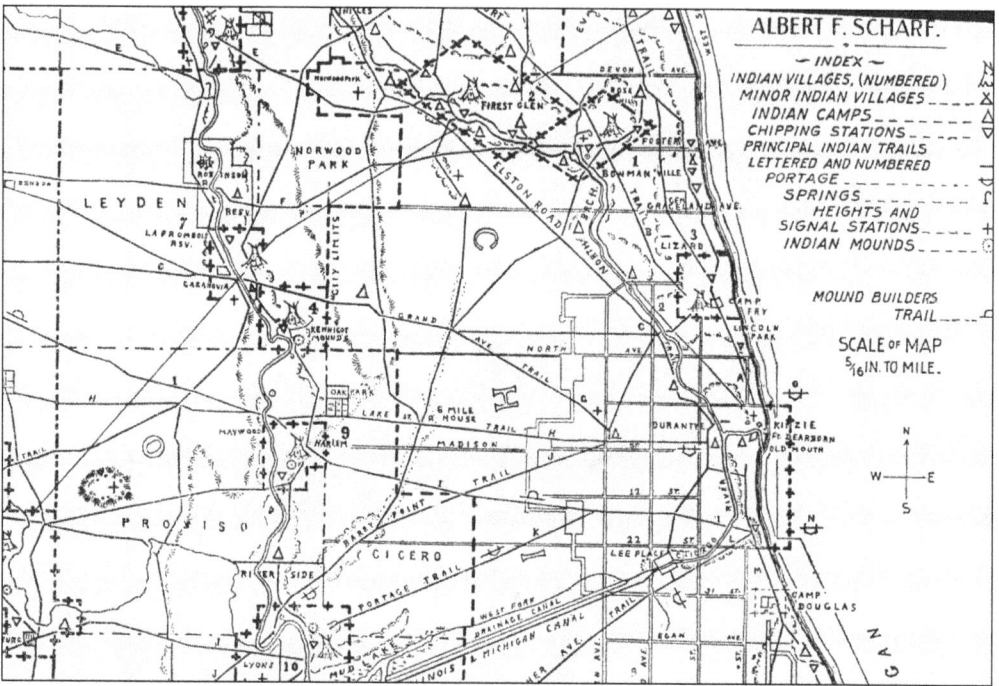

ALBERT F. SCHARF.

— INDEX —
INDIAN VILLAGES, (NUMBERED)
MINOR INDIAN VILLAGES _ _ _ _
INDIAN CAMPS _ _ _ _ _ _ _
CHIPPING STATIONS _ _ _ _ _
PRINCIPAL INDIAN TRAILS
LETTERED AND NUMBERED
PORTAGE _ _ _ _ _ _ _ _
SPRINGS _ _ _ _ _ _ _ _
HEIGHTS AND
SIGNAL STATIONS _ _ _ _
INDIAN MOUNDS _ _ _ _ _

MOUND BUILDERS
TRAIL _ _ _

SCALE of MAP
5⁄16 IN. TO MILE.

This map, drawn by Albert F. Scharf, shows that in 1804, the entire southern portion of Elmwood Park was considered a Native American signal station. There was a chipping station in what is now Evans Field, and the Kennicott Mounds were located about 300 yards north of North Avenue, just north of where Russell's parking lot is now. Unfortunately, the ancient mounds no longer exist.

The scene depicted in this postcard is similar to the curve the Des Plaines River makes in the area just above North Avenue. The river made this site an important one to the Native Americans. However, after the spring floods subsided, the river would often be unnavigable. Dams built later along the river, especially in Riverside, kept the river at an unnaturally high level. (Author's collection.)

This is the Rhodes-Marwood farmhouse, which B. Rhodes sold to Fryer Marwood. The house stood for over 115 years before being replaced by an apartment building. The Jehovah's Witness Kingdom Hall, which was instituted in 1940, lies just west of where this house stood.

The old "48" was one of the first locomotives to pull trains through what is now Elmwood Park and across what was Marwood's farm. The steam engine was known as an "American Type" 4-4-0. The number designation refers to the wheel arrangement. This one, built in 1865, was one of 25,000 manufactured. By the turn of the century, they were considered obsolete. Today, only about 40 survive. (Courtesy of Elmwood Park High School.)

This home once belonged to John Gnaedinger and his wife, Alma. John was born in Lexington, Kentucky, and he and his cousin Henry became active in the local real estate market. The home, seen here in 1892, was built around 1890 at Harrison and Princeton Streets, which are known today as Seventy-third Court and Altgeld Street, respectively. The structure was razed in the early 1960s.

Neighbors Mae Schumacher (left), Robert Gnaedinger, and his stepsister Elizabeth Meness look quite fashionable as they pose on the porch of the Gnaedinger home around 1890. Robert's well-dressed appearance suggests a special event and also gives an indication of the family's wealth. In 1964, Elizabeth was looking forward to the village's golden jubilee, but she passed away a month shy of the celebration. She would have been the oldest surviving pioneer.

The John C. Schumacher house at 2530 North Seventy-second Court lost many of its embellishments and ornate trim over the years. The house looked much different in its prime (see page 15). It was sided sometime before this 1960 picture was taken. The home was severely damaged in a fire on February 9, 1988. It was later demolished and replaced by apartment buildings.

The isolation of Louis Longfield's farm in 1912 stands in stark contrast to the congestion that encompasses the area at Harlem and Schubert Avenues today. The old homestead at 2640 Harlem Avenue has since been replaced with apartment buildings. Otto Longfield, Louis's brother, had his own farm a bit farther north on Harlem Avenue.

Another of the early large Victorian homes was this one, built by Charles Last in the unincorporated section of Leyden Township. At the time, Leyden was known as Orison, Illinois. The home, at Lovett Avenue near Princeton Street, was reportedly moved north of Atlgeld Avenue. Sadly, this structure and many of its contemporaries met the wrecking ball and were replaced with apartment buildings.

The early development of the village can be attributed in large part to the Grand Avenue streetcar line, which was extended to Harlem Avenue in 1911. The streetcar brought eager homebuyers from the dirty and crowded inner city, seeking fresh air and open spaces as the land was quickly subdivided and developed. This view is looking east on Grand Avenue at Nordica Avenue in 1916.

The home that stands at 2704 North Seventy-second Court still looks much as it does in this 1960 photograph. It is the last surviving Victorian building in an area that once housed many of the town's oldest homes. The house was built in 1890 by Theodore and Anna Sanchez. Theodore was born in Iowa in 1849. His son Frank served five years as the village treasurer.

John C. Schumacher built this house at Lovett Avenue and Princeton Street (now Seventy-second Court and Altgeld Street) in 1890, when the town was still known as Orison. Schumacher was a real estate partner of the Gnaedinger cousins, John and Henry. Together, they built the first subdivision, Marwood Park. Schumacher's closest neighbors were the Gnaedingers and the Ellsworths. He sold the home around the time of incorporation to village trustee Fred Reckendorf.

This 1903 map of Leyden Township shows how the land had been subdivided over the years. The "developed" section of what is now Elmwood Park was called Ellsworth. Its boundaries were Diversey, Harlem, Fullerton and Eightieth Avenues (Webster). Note the Elmwood Brook and various lakes that existed in the Elmwood Cemetery. There was also an entrance at what would be the intersection of Sunset Drive and Grand Avenue. (Courtesy of University of Chicago Library.)

The home in this 1960s photograph was located on the east side of the 2500 block of Seventy-second Court. It was built by Henry Gnaedinger in 1892 and was once owned by William Graham, the first police magistrate of the village. Graham served in that role from 1914 until 1919. This home stood for nearly 100 years, until it was demolished in 1987 and replaced with apartment buildings.

John Burmeister, shown here in 1914, would leave the farm he rented from James McGawn at midnight, four days a week, and travel along Grand Avenue to sell his produce at the market on West Randolph Street. The trip took four hours each way. The 80-acre farm, located at Harlem and Belmont Avenues, was initially a part of the village at incorporation. Burmeister is credited with killing the last timber wolf in the area, at Seventy-fourth and Belmont Avenues.

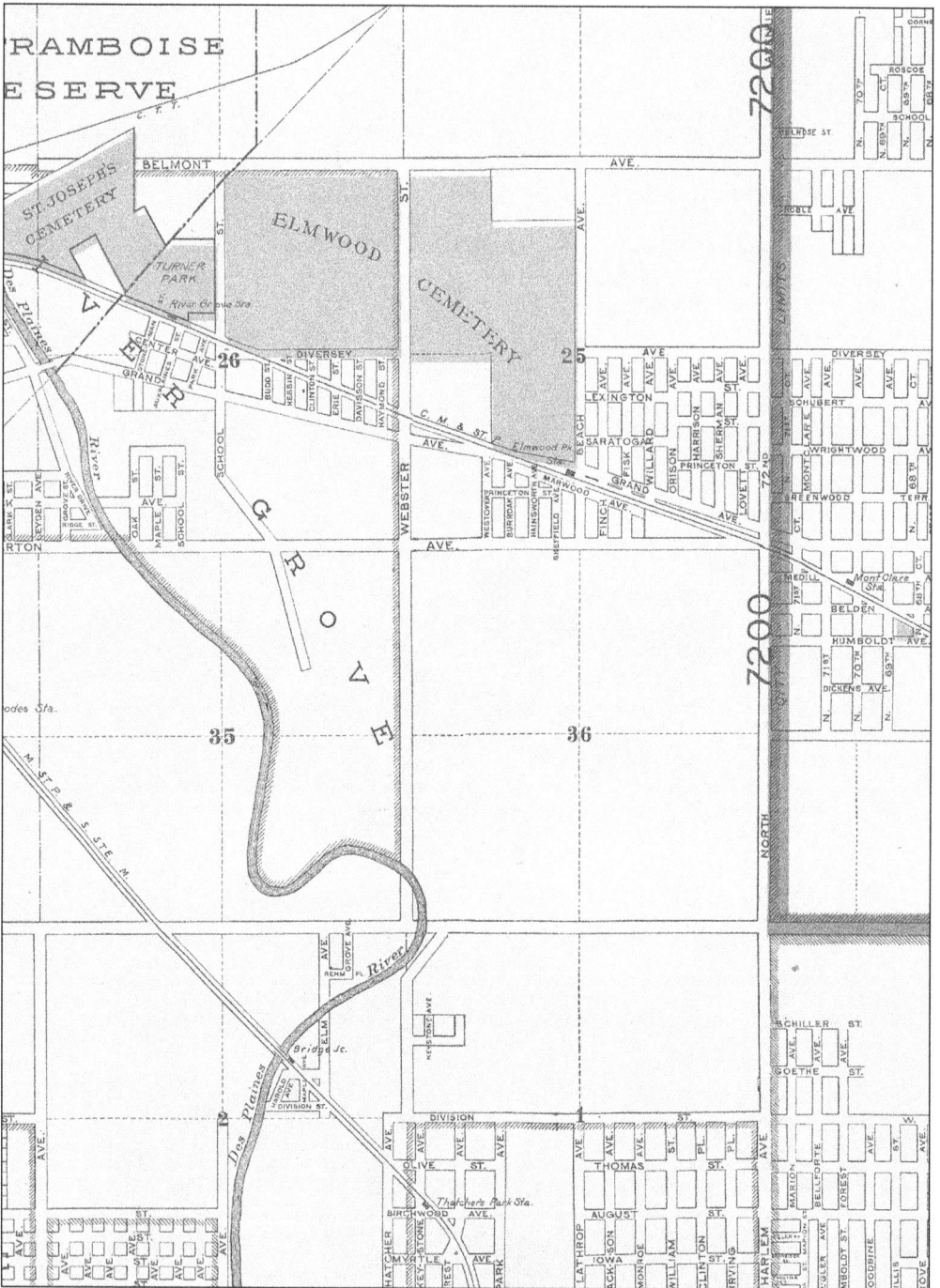

This map from 1910 also shows the vast expanse of what was the original Elmwood Cemetery. It is interesting to note that almost all of the development in the area was limited to the east half of the southwest and the entire southeast quarter of Section 25, encompassing all 240 acres originally purchased by James H. Rees in 1836. Also, note that the train station already bore the name Elmwood Park when this map was drawn. (Courtesy of University of Chicago Library.)

18

Two

GROWTH

Beginning in the late 1890s, developers saw the potential of this area. Soon, real estate agents set up tents and offices at Harlem and Grand Avenues to catch people as they came out from the city to visit loved ones interred at Elmwood Cemetery or to breathe fresh country air in the groves along the river.

This area has been known by many names. It was called Orison (also Orrison), Ellsworth, and unincorporated Leyden Township. By 1903, there was a station on the Chicago, Milwaukee & St. Paul Railroad called Elmwood Park.

As the community grew, talk of incorporation began. On March 24, 1914, an election was held, and the motion to incorporate was passed. On April 8, 1914, Judge Owens entered the order incorporating the village. That same month, the village lost a court battle, as well as the northeast portion of the village, southwest of Harlem and Belmont Avenues, which is part of Chicago today.

The first major subdivision, on the south end of town, was called Green Fields. Begun by Mills & Son, its boundaries were North Avenue on the south, Harlem Avenue on the east, Armitage Avenue on the north, and Seventy-eighth Avenue on the west. Green Fields offered 280 half-acre lots for between $600 and $800. The Green Fields project would be considered small just a few years later when, in 1926, Mills & Son purchased 243 acres of the Elmwood Cemetery that had not been used for burial purposes, for about $2,500 an acre. Their goal was to build 600 to 700 homes a year, for three years.

Slowed by the Great Depression, these and other building projects had a tremendous impact on the population of the village, creating a need for churches, schools, and business. Of all the homes in the village today, only 45 were built before 1915, and only 3 remain from the 1800s.

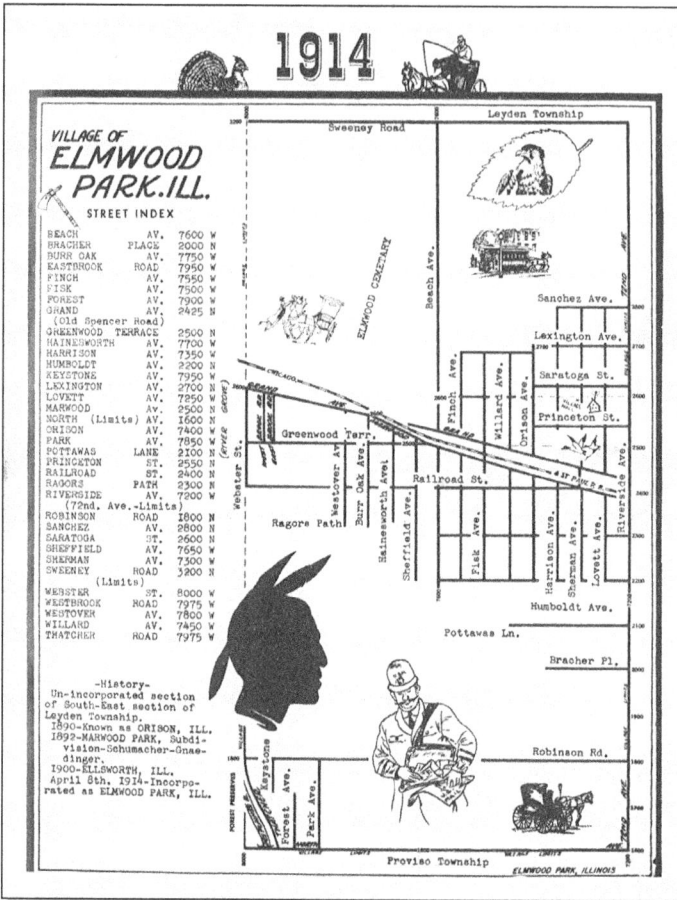

This map shows how the village looked at the time of incorporation. The boundaries extended northeast to Harlem and Belmont Avenues. Closer inspection shows the location of the first village hall, in addition to long-forgotten street names, which were relabeled in 1921.

This is the only known image of the original Elmwood Park Village Hall. The small wood-frame structure was dedicated on October 3, 1914, at 2536 Sherman Avenue (Seventy-third Avenue), just south of Saratoga Street (Wrightwood) on land donated by Fred A. Reckendorf. It served until a new municipal building was erected in 1928. The original village hall was torn down in 1931. (*Tribune* photograph.)

Members of the first Village Board of Elmwood Park pose in 1914. Shown here are, from left to right, (first row) Walter L. Schumacher (clerk), John A Peterson, Carl E. Holm, Charles Grimm, and William A. Graham (police magistrate); (second row) Henry Hermann, Fred A Reckendorf, Katherine Phelan, Carl E Johnson Jr. (president), and Peter W. Richling. Phelan had the distinction of being elected six years prior to the passage of the Nineteenth Amendment, which guaranteed women the right to vote.

Elmwood School was the first school in the village. The four-room facility was built in 1914 at what was then called Finch Street and Fullerton Avenue. The increasing population created a need for expansion, and another four rooms were added. This explains the different roofing styles in the photograph. A much larger addition, built in 1958, formed an L shape around the older structures. These older sections were razed in 1971.

21

Tent sales, like this one at the northwest corner of Grand and Harlem Avenues, found a receptive audience of people venturing out of the city on excursions. In 1915, the Volk Brothers, along with E.A. Cummings, were successful developers of the area. Their names, along with that of Mills, still appear on the legal descriptions of the individual parcels that make up the village.

Volk Brothers was one of the first real estate brokers to sell lots in the newly formed Elmwood Park. The brothers benefited from the village's prime location at the end of the Grand Avenue streetcar line. In those days, both Harlem and Grand Avenues were little more than dirt roads that became muddy paths during the rainy seasons.

This daring young chap, strolling atop the rails while enjoying a smoke, is a member of the local baseball team. The team was most likely the Elmwood AC (Athletic Club), which was a member of the Chicago Junior Baseball League in 1916. The league featured teams from all over the area, including the Berwyn Feds and the Ridgelands.

Otto Longfield is seen on his farm at George Street and Harlem Avenue in 1915. Before it was known as Harlem Avenue, the road was called Townline Road, Seventy-second Avenue, and even Riverside Avenue. In 1915, Longfield loaned the village $1,000 to help get it started, and he became a village trustee. His brother Louis lived at 2640 Harlem Avenue and his nephew Ralph resided at 2636 Harlem Avenue.

One Of The Beautiful Concrete And Steel Entrances To. "GREEN FIELDS"

MILLS & SON
3656 NORTH AVE
ALL Phones. BELMONT 1501.

The Green Fields subdivision covered the area bounded by North Avenue to the south, Harlem Avenue to the east, Armitage Avenue on the north, and Seventy-eighth Avenue on the west. Situated between the Oak Park Country Club and the Westward Ho Golf Club, the development was marked by entrance gates at North Avenue and Seventy-second Court and at Seventy-second (Harlem) Avenue and Cortland Street. Half-acre lots (133 feet by 133 feet) sold for between $600 and $800.

The model home featured in this 1915 rendering of the Green Fields subdivision was located at 1850 North Harlem Avenue. Austrian-born Joseph "Papa" Horwath Sr. opened a restaurant, which was considered a blind pig, or speakeasy, in the building in 1931. The restaurant featured a large and varied menu for both lunch and dinner. Generations dined on such delicacies as veal Oscar, lobster Collens, and Philadelphia pepper steak.

24

By 1917, the intersection of Harlem and Grand Avenues was already a center of activity. This view looking north on Harlem Avenue from the tracks shows several jitney buses ready to take passengers from the streetcars to Elmwood or St Joseph's Cemeteries or perhaps to the woods for a picnic. The buses, a cross between a taxi and a bus, carried eight to ten passengers for a nickel each.

This photograph of the July 4, 1915, entertainment committee was taken in a field at Seventy-sixth and Armitage Avenues, near the current site of Centennial Park. The rather formally dressed group consists of, from left to right, (first row) unidentified, Mrs. Charles Thompson, and unidentified; (second row) John Keeney, H. Ardnt, Henry Christie, Herman Eterwin, Louis Longfield, and Peter D. McArthur. Thompson was the daughter of Fred Reckendorf.

Police officer Max Miller is seen around 1917 astride his Excelsior motorcycle in front of the pool hall on Grand Avenue near Harlem Avenue. The Excelsior Company, owned by the Schwinn corporation, was the preferred maker of vehicles for law enforcement in 1916. The company was once one of the three main motorcycle manufacturers, along with Indian and Harley-Davidson.

The year was 1918 when Ed Peters and his wife, Minnie, took this photograph with a little neighbor girl named Blanche on their farm at Thatcher Road near Bloomingdale Avenue. They later moved to a home at 2512 North Seventy-second Court. Minnie served as the police matron, taking care of any women or children who were locked up in the village jail. Their horse looks like it has seen better days.

Patriotism was the order of the day during World War I, as evidenced by the American flags in the windows of Herb Kuhagen's Elmwood Pool Hall. The establishment was located next door to the first tavern in the village, the Gold Mine, which was built by Sam Arado. That building, on the northwest corner, was later home to Ablin's Drugstore for over 50 years.

In this interior photograph of Herbert Kuhagen's Elmwood Pool Hall, note the mud-splattered stools, which illustrate the poor conditions of both Grand and Harlem Avenues. The mud was often so bad that people would remove their boots and stash them in a local business before boarding the streetcars to go into the city.

Siblings Dorothy and Ernest Sanders are seen on their family farm on the south end of Elmwood Park near Wabansia Avenue. This photograph was taken in the early 1920s, just before Lake Michigan water began to be supplied to the village. Although Elmwood Park benefited from a high water table and many underground springs, the water quality was poor. Only a few dwellings dot the field in the distance.

An Elmwood School classroom is seen here in the 1920s. The population explosion, along with the lack of parochial schools, led to large class sizes. The students here represent several grades. Teachers made an average of $800 per year, which equates to about $52,000 today.

28

(1920)

On Palm Sunday, March 28, 1920, a destructive tornado passed through the northwest section of the village at approximately 1:00 p.m. Originating about 1.5 miles north of Channahon, it traveled 50 miles northeast, hitting Melrose Park at about 12:55 and ending at the lake near Wilmette. The death toll included ten people in Melrose Park and six in Dunning. Here, it struck Phillip Schaeffer's farm just north of Belmont Avenue between Seventy-sixth and Eightieth Avenues.

This 1921 photograph shows the local baseball team posing in front of a billboard promoting 450 new homes under construction. The players are, from left to right, (first row) Oscar Peters, John "Lefty" Cawthorne, a Mr. Geyer, and "Frenchy"; (second row) Ole Olsen, Herb Kuhagen, Clarence Boerstal, and two unidentified players. Kuhagen was also owner of the local pool hall.

This Keystone Country Club advertisement from the 1930s seems to welcome all. The members-only club, owned by Al Goodiell, was the scene of a gambling raid in July 1918. A constable from Oak Park was met by 20 sluggers who reportedly beat him up, stripped him of his gun, and threw him out of the club. The Keystone closed in the late 1930s.

The Keystone Club was a speakeasy/social club located just south of the Oak Park Country Club, east of Thatcher Avenue. The club included the gondola launch seen in this c. 1920 photograph, west of Thatcher Avenue on the east bank of the Des Plaines River. The occasionally rowdy nature of the club patrons did not sit well with the members of the neighboring Oak Park Country Club.

Sunset Drive is one of the oldest roads in the Westwood subdivision. Before development began, the thoroughfare served as the eastern access road from Grand Avenue into the Elmwood Cemetery. The road still terminates at the gates along Eightieth Avenue. The graceful arc of the road inspired the developers to create the curved Elmgrove and Cressett Drives and Oakleaf and Birchdale Avenues, which are unique to that section of town.

The open fields and farmland presented relief to those struggling to feed their families in 1929. The area was prime hunting ground for swamp rabbits. The hunters seen here are, from left to right, Tony Alagna, J. Jerfith, Peter Tibreri, and two unidentified men. The men are displaying the spoils of the hunt outside of 2444 North Harlem Avenue.

Jack Mills of Mills & Sons proudly stands front and center with construction foremen during the golden year of 1927. The company, however, failed a few years later. In 1932, the firm was placed in receivership for money owed the Hydraulic Press Brick Company, one of nearly 50 unsecured creditors. The company officially declared bankruptcy in 1933.

The Mills & Sons construction crews were kept busy in the years 1927–1929, when they completed over 1,500 brick bungalows in Westwood. At times, they were completing the homes at a rate of four a day. A five-room house could be purchased for $8,950, or $500 down and $55 a month. Each home featured hardwood floors and its own garage adjacent to freshly paved alleys. There were 10 different models, and no two homes on a block were identical.

This residence, at 3119 North Seventy-seventh Court, was once the home of local historian Frank Vesper. The house is a good example of a Mills bungalow. The characteristic that sets these homes apart from other Chicago-style bungalows are the Louis Sullivan–styled, ornamental terra-cotta tiles that adorn the brick facades. The tiles used to accent the window surrounds and entrances were made by the Midland Terra Cotta Company of Chicago.

An Ideal Community of Completed Homes

Garage and Back Yard Hedge Fencing of WESTWOOD *Homes*

If this artist's rendering looks familiar to those who live, or have lived, in the historic Westwood section of town, it is because it comes from a Mills & Sons sales brochure. In it, the company states that hedges will separate the lots, and fencing with gates will line the alleys. In a time when owning a car seemed more like a luxury than a necessity, single-car garages sufficed.

This 1926 photograph gives some perspective to the immensity of the Westwood development. It shows some of the sewer pipes waiting to be installed. The photographer is looking northwest from Seventy-sixth Avenue. In the distance is a portion of the Schaeffer farm, located near Belmont Avenue (see page 29). The line of trees in the distance is probably along Eightieth Avenue.

This 1928 view of Oakleaf Avenue could be mistaken for a recent scene, but note the vintage car and the small parkway trees. The occasional flooding that occurs in the area may be due to Elmwood Brook, which once ran from as far north as Belmont Avenue, down along Eightieth Avenue between East and West Brook Roads, before terminating at the grounds of the Oak Park Country Club.

This postcard touting the benefits of living in Westwood shows the French fountain in its prime. The fountain, which was the centerpiece of the five-acre park, was 22 feet in diameter and had a 15-foot-high pedestal. The park and fountain were donated to the village by John Mills and dedicated to his wife, Lottie, with the stipulation that the park remain free of development and be accessible to the people. (Author's collection.)

First E.P. Library

During construction of Westwood, salesmen used these touring cars to show prospective buyers around the neighborhood. The view in this photograph looks north from Seventy-sixth and Grand Avenues. The Mills sales office, seen on the left, would eventually become the first public library. The fountain can be seen in the distance, as it was not much smaller than the newly planted trees that surrounded it.

This postcard, another in a series promoting Westwood, shows Sunset Drive. The street is nearly devoid of cars. When Westwood was built, it was a luxury to own one car, let alone two. Today's homeowners often find the original one-car garages woefully inadequate and have replaced many of them with two-car garages. (Author's collection.)

This real-photo postcard features the Westwood Bank. At the time, it was one of only a couple of commercial buildings that existed around the perimeter of the Circle. The Westwood Bank failed in 1932, but the building still stands. It is a visually interesting structure, as the architects mirrored the graceful curves of the Circle and surrounding streets by curving the building. (Author's collection.)

The large number of trains passing through the village makes automobile and train collisions an all-too-frequent occurrence, often with tragic results. Three Elmwood Park musicians—Joe Bates, Harry Bessinger, and Walter Herman—met an untimely end when a Milwaukee Road train struck their car at the Seventy-third Avenue crossing in 1924. The driver, Bessinger, was reportedly buried with the missing part of the steering wheel.

This 1930 aerial rendering of the Westwood development is interesting on a couple of levels. Visible at upper center, along Seventy-sixth Avenue, is the large undeveloped tract between Wellington and Barry Avenues. It is also remarkable to see the open spaces in the Belmont Heights area of Chicago, just north of Belmont Avenue, as well as the area south of the tracks.

John Mills School, located at 2824 North Seventy-sixth Avenue, has suffered growing pains over the years. Built in 1929, the school, seen here on November 19, 1946, served 863 students. An eight-room addition was built in 1947 to accommodate the baby boomers. In the 1970s, the school required three mobile classrooms.

Northway Homes, Inc. created this advertisement for "charming homes" in River Forest Manor, using that moniker to describe the south end of town. Several years earlier, that area was known as Green Fields. The name change was likely an attempt to capitalize on the perceived affluence of the neighbor to the south. This development consisted of 300 homesites. The houses were built to order by Fredrickson & Company.

$300 Starts You
to ownership of one of these
CHARMING HOMES

IF you're bound to have a lovely home, plus the advantage of an ideal location, and all modern improvements in and paid for—this is THE remarkable purchasing opportunity! Fine large lots, out of the high tax district, are the setting for these beautiful homes. You have easy access to Oak Park and Grand-Harlem shopping centers—street car, steam, and elevated transportation, and excellent schools and churches.

River Forest Manor

$39⁴⁷ PER MO.

F. H. A. plan makes it easy for you to own your home with less money than you pay for rent. Drive out today—see our new Model Home on the property. You'll want to make River Forest Manor your home.

Phone
LAC.
9671

Northway Homes Inc.
Office—1940 N. Harlem Ave., Cor. Armitage 4 blocks north of North Ave.

38

Three

VILLAGE LIFE

This chapter roughly follows the years 1930 to 1953. During this time, the population of the village nearly doubled. Although the Depression caused Mills & Sons to seek bankruptcy protection, the homes built by the firm continued to sell. Vacant bungalows sold for $3,500.

With the coming of World War II, the village did its part, sending hundreds of young men into battle. Several would not return, including S.Sgt. Guy Joseph Conti, who was killed at Guadalcanal, and Forrest O. Rednour, a Coast Guard cook second class who rescued 133 men after his ship exploded. The USS *Rednour* was named for him. There was also 1st Lt. Ralph Halbrook, an Army ace who destroyed 32 enemy planes. The village even scrapped its war memorial, an artillery gun, for the war effort. Those who did return home started families and businesses.

The resultant baby boom filled the town's schools to such an extent that a new elementary school, named Elm, was built on the south side of the village to accommodate the growing number of students. Several churches were built or enlarged during the period as well. The Harlem and Grand Avenue shopping area reached the peak of its popularity.

Around this time, many Italian Americans began moving out of the old neighborhoods in Chicago to the suburbs. It was here that they found room for their expanding families and space to grow fruits and vegetables in backyards of their own. Once here, they opened restaurants and shops that catered to their ethnic background and heritage.

The first structure to house St. Celestine Parish was this Mills bungalow at the northeast corner of Wellington Avenue and Seventy-sixth Court. Father Shea, the first pastor, stands in front of the house, which is still used as accommodations for visiting clergy The structure served the "only miniature parish church in America" until a larger church was built across the street. The home still displays a telltale crucifix above one of the doorways.

This crowd has gathered for St. Celestine's second open-air mission, on Sunday, September 11, 1938. The mission was open to all who wanted to witness the teachings of the Catholic Church. In the background is the first church built on the current site. The combination church, school, and auditorium was constructed immediately after the first open-air mission was held in 1932. The last outdoor mission took place in 1939.

In July 1928, the police department used this interesting vehicle, outfitted with rugged rear tires, to gather stray dogs. From left to right are driver Tony Ross, Police Chief Ted Schuette, and Lt. Henry Trapp. Stray dogs were a common problem in the days before imbedded microchips, as most homes were not entirely fenced in.

The Oak Park Country Club, which opened in 1914, is located in River Grove, but actually straddles the boundary with Elmwood Park. In 1954, the club sold 106 acres to the Elmwood Park High School district for the construction of Elmwood Park High School. The architect for the clubhouse, seen on this postcard, was Norman S. Patton, who was also the chairman of the private club. Many local teens spent summers as caddies at the club. (Author's collection.)

The Goodyear airship *Puritan* made an appearance on the south end of town near North Avenue, probably during the Century of Progress World's Fair, held in Chicago in 1933–1934. The 128-foot-long airship had a maximum speed of 55 miles per hour and could carry up to six passengers. Hydrogen gas, the deadly component of the airship *Hindenburg* disaster, had been replaced with 86,000 cubic feet of helium.

The Elmwood Park police force is seen here in 1929. Shown here are, from left to right, John Kvistad (village clerk), Lt. Henry Trapp, Edward Ambrose, Chief Frank Rice, Capt. Edward Woods, Lt. Ed Winters, ? Smith, Nels Christy, Lou Shaw, and village president Charley Hoehamer. Chief Rice served until 1951. Motorcycle officer Nels Christy was killed in the line of duty in August 1930, when his motorcycle was struck by a truck at Seventy-seventh and Diversey Avenues.

This c. 1929 postcard shows Elmwood Park State Bank, located at 7201 Grand Avenue. The building was briefly the home of the Elmwood Park Public Library in 1938–1939. Later, the structure's brick exterior was covered during a renovation. The building was destroyed by fire in 1983. The site is currently home to Dunkin' Donuts.

The Lewis Funeral Home, 7600 Grand Avenue, was a place where many villagers said their final good-byes to friends and loved ones. Once known as the Murphy Funeral Home, the building was in the process of being sold when a fire damaged the landmark structure on March 19, 2009. A group with strong village ties built a new funeral home, The Elms, which opened the following spring on the same site.

The Elm Theatre, located at 7532 West Grand Avenue, was a single-screen, 700-seat Art Deco facility built in 1937. It closed in 1960 and became the Elm Bargain Mart for a few years. The facade was demolished in 1965, and the auditorium became an Armanetti's liquor store and, later, a hardware store. The auditorium is the only portion of the building that remains.

While most of the grand movie palaces were classically inspired, the Art Deco styling of the time was carried through to the interior of the Elm Theatre. The Elm's lobby is seen here when the theater first opened. After the theater closed, moviegoers had to travel a few blocks east, to the Mont Clare Theatre. Today, the closest movie theater is the Cinemark in Melrose Park.

The John Mills School graduating class of 1946 may not have had any professional actors, but the students did get a chance to appear on stage at the Elm Theatre. That is where this photograph was taken. Some movies that came out that year would have made great themes for the occasion, such as *The Best Years of Our Lives*, *It's a Wonderful Life*, and *Great Expectations*.

Construction began in 1929 on the building known as Grace Lutheran Church, at 2700 North Harlem Avenue. The congregation, originally named Messiah Lutheran Church, was formed when two missions, the Faith Mission and the Hope Mission, merged in 1920. The name was changed to Grace Lutheran in 1935. A school building was erected adjacent to the church in 1951. The congregation was bolstered in 2000, when it merged with the Westwood Lutheran Church. (Author's photograph.)

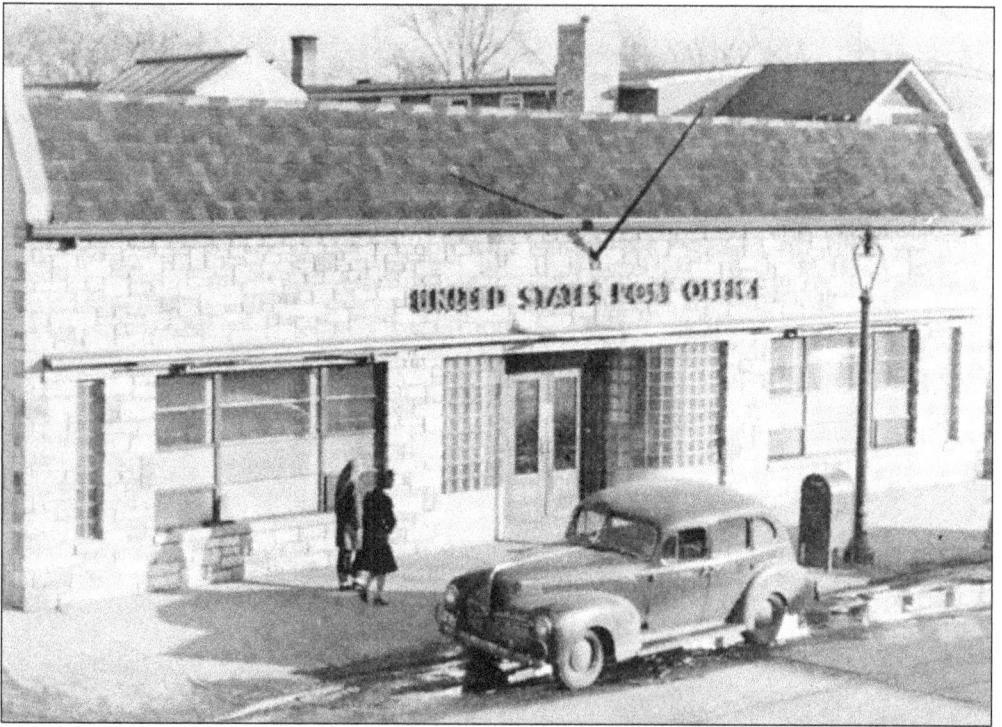

Although located on the Chicago side of Harlem Avenue, this building, at 2515 Harlem Avenue, served for many years as Elmwood Park's post office. In an elaborately planned raid in 1952, five armed men stole three packages, only to find they contained financial records and cancelled checks. Their only score was the $35 they took from a cash drawer. The building has been home to the Royal Gardens Banquet Hall since the late 1960s.

The children of 1942 faced an uncertain future. The war was far from over, and its outcome was not at all certain. Families had to deal with rationing and with homes without fathers, uncles, brothers, and cousins. Three months after this photograph was taken, the first service flag flew at the village hall. It had 400 stars, representing the men who had left to fight the war.

46

The *Hiawatha* — FIRST OF THE SPEEDLINERS — THE MILWAUKEE ROAD

The *Hiawatha* locomotive passed through town daily at 1:07 p.m. during the 1940s. The streamlined orange, black, and silver locomotive, which was operated by the Chicago, Milwaukee, St. Paul & Pacific Railroad, was so punctual that people could set their watches by it. The train, which usually had between 10 and 14 coaches, had a self-imposed speed limit of 100 miles per hour. (Author's collection.)

This aerial photograph of the Circle, taken on June 1, 1946, by Rodger Hammill, shows the West Grand Avenue grade crossing, which has been the scene of 45 accidents between 1956 and 2005. These accidents resulted in 7 fatalities and 27 injuries. Most notable was the Thanksgiving eve accident of 2005, in which a Metra train collided with 18 motor vehicles. The crossing, at 366 feet, is the widest in the state.

47

For years, this drill tower stood behind the municipal building. In 1946, some 600 suburban firefighters from 75 villages and volunteer fire departments learned such critical skills as jumping techniques, lowering stretchers, and rope rescues as part of a fire school organized by Elmwood Park fire chief Chester Reardon and River Forest chief A.F. Zay. Judging by the cars, this photograph was taken in the late 1950s or early 1960s.

On Christmas Eve 1939, Santa traded in his famous sleigh and eight tiny reindeer for a ride on one of Elmwood Park's fire trucks. The firemen helped Santa distribute candy to the children during the height of the Depression, bringing some much-needed joy at a very difficult time for most families. The tradition was halted for the duration of World War II, but resumed when the war ended.

The uniquely shaped and highly decorative bank at 7302 Grand Avenue is seen here in the 1940s. It later housed restaurants and was the scene of a tremendous fire in April 1975. The incident nearly turned tragic, as several firefighters barely escaped as the roof collapsed. The fire, which began in the Cathay Mandarin Restaurant, also destroyed the Villa Roma Restaurant. The blaze was ruled accidental.

This is another classic aerial photograph by Rodger Hammill from 1946. This viewpoint is from above the south side of Grand Avenue, looking east. Note the Y shape that begins just east of Harlem as the tracks veer south and Grand Avenue takes a northeasterly route. The Rhodes/Marwood house can just be seen among a dark thicket of trees right of center. (Courtesy of the Franklin Park Library.)

Members of the John Mills School class of 1939 look like Ivy Leaguers in this graduation photograph. Despite the fact that the darkest days of the Depression were over, the young scholars faced an uncertain future. Since Elmwood Park had no high school of its own, the classmates would go their separate ways, and some would undoubtedly be headed to the service, as World War II was just around the corner.

Proviso High School, located at First Avenue and Madison Street, was one of nine area high schools that Elmwood Park students attended. Other schools included Leyden, Steinmetz, Oak Park River Forest, and parochial high schools. Notable alumni of Proviso include Elmer Conti and Ray Nitschke. (Author's collection.)

St. Celestine's parish grew quickly, and it became clear that the eight-room school built at the back of the church would have to be replaced. In 1945, some 345 children filled the building so fully that one sister had no room for her own desk. In June 1946, ground was broken for a new school, convent, and auditorium. By the time the 17-classroom school opened in September 1947, the enrollment had nearly doubled, to 650 children.

This sprawling Georgian-style home at 2101 North Seventy-sixth Court was built by Kenneth Idle, who owned a Chrysler Plymouth dealership at 8201 West Grand Avenue in the 1940s and 1950s. Since the 1940s, when this photograph was taken, the home, which fronts Dickens Avenue, has lost the majestic trees that once surrounded it.

This Hammill photograph, looking north on Harlem Avenue, was taken on July 20, 1946. With nearly all of Harlem Avenue consisting of empty lots or single-family homes, in hindsight, this would have been the time to widen the busy thoroughfare. Cruising that stretch of road was a popular weekend activity for area teenagers looking to show off their wheels. (Courtesy of the Franklin Park Library.)

In another bird's-eye view of the Grand Avenue shopping district taken by Hammill in 1946, streetcars can be seen hitting the end of the line at Harlem Avenue. Popular stores of the time are visible, such as the A&P Food Mart and Sabath's department store, located across Harlem in Mont Clare. On the Elmwood Park side is Windmiller's, which, following a merger the following year, became Alden's Windmiller. (Courtesy of the Franklin Park Library.)

This 1947 photograph shows a gathering of local political heavyweights. Pictured are, from left to right, John Cullerton (Elmwood Park president), Barry Reeves (Franklin Park mayor), Arthur J. Bidwell (state senator from River Forest), and Harry Smith (River Grove mayor). Cullerton was the third-longest-serving village president (1935–1948).

Charles Strausser is seen in 1947 tending to his garden at Belden Avenue and Seventy-second Court. Many suburbanites started gardens during the war years as victory or "war" gardens. The government encouraged gardening to help reduce the cost of produce needed to feed the troops. An apartment building now stands on the site of the garden, at 2300 North Seventy-second Court. (Courtesy of Shelia Severino.)

The United Methodist church, located at 3000 North Seventy-seventh Court, was begun in 1928. The church itself was built in 1935 and rebuilt in 1947. The cupola was removed from the Federal Colonial building in 2012, and the church is now also used by the Out of the Box ministry.

Based on the amount of snow in this photograph of St. Celestine's, it may have been taken after the blizzard of 1967. The Lannon stone facade actually hides a smaller wood-frame church below the surface. The building had been enlarged in 1941 and covered with the stone. The home visible to the right of the old church was demolished during construction of the current church. (Courtesy of St. Celestine's.)

The Westwood Evangelical Lutheran Church, at 7810 Elmgrove Drive, was organized on October 12, 1928. With a diminishing congregation, the church decided to unite with Grace Lutheran in 2000. The building stood empty for a year before the New Horizon Temple moved in. The new congregation, which is a part of the United Pentecostal Church, has restored portions of the church and added a much-needed parking lot.

Zoar Lutheran Church, 2940 North Seventy-fifth Court, was organized on December 31, 1927. The church, part of the Missouri Synod, is one of two Lutheran churches left in the village. The building was erected in 1930 and a school was later added. In the past few years, the church has been active in the Toys for Tots program and other community activities.

The intersection of Grand and Harlem Avenues has always been a hub of activity and a key component to the economic prosperity of the village. As such, the location has always been in a constant state of evolution. The hustle and bustle continues today, but the only building still standing from this 1949 photograph is the home of the Italo-American Soccer Club, Maroons, located at 7209 West Grand Avenue. The view faces southwest.

The Goldblatts store at 2430 North Harlem Avenue was the 16th store in the chain, which at its peak numbered 20. The discount retailer opened in November 1948 and closed on March 21, 1981, as part of its bankruptcy. Visible at far right is the 250-foot-tall radio tower, erected in 1948 to transmit 107.1 FM, later 105.9 FM. The transmitter was later moved to the Sears Tower.

The ground breaking for the Elm School took place on April 10, 1948. The grand affair was filled with patriotism, bands, and prominent officials. Among the dignitaries present was Ralph Orison Longfield, a member of one of earliest and most well-known families in the area. The school was completed in 1949. Note how the area around the school still appears to be quite rural at the time. (Courtesy of Shelia Severino.)

The Mercury Theatre, 7230 North Avenue, was the village's second cinema. The 1,198-seat theater opened on December 30, 1949, and was purchased in the 1950s by Balaban & Katz. It was sold in the 1970s to the Plitt Theatre Group, which divided the theater in the 1980s. It was closed in 1988 by its owner, Cineplex Odeon, and demolished. The site is now occupied by a strip mall, which was anchored by, ironically enough, a Blockbuster Video store until it closed in November 2013.

Maintaining a healthy canopy of trees has been a challenge as well as a top priority for the public works department. In the 1950s, the village purchased a multiuse vehicle, seen here as a tree is trimmed in front of 2947 North Seventy-fourth Avenue. The adjustable platform provided a safe way to reach high into the mature trees.

Many returning war veterans delighted in working on their own cars. As the hot rod era began, auto-parts stores such as Speed's, located at 7450 Grand Avenue, began springing up. While most of the old store was demolished to make way for a gas station, a portion of the building remains as part of the BP station that is presently at that location

Ground breaking for the south fire station at 7420 Fullerton Avenue occurred on October 21, 1950. The fire barn was needed to service the south side of the village due to its rapid growth and because of the trains that could delay firefighters coming from the municipal building. This photograph was probably taken in the early 1960s. The ambulance looks like the Ecto-1 1959 Cadillac featured in the film *Ghostbusters*.

This view looking southeast toward Seventy-seventh Court was taken from the Chicago side of Belmont Avenue. The Williams Department Store no longer exists, but the building has been home to the Elmwood Family restaurant since 1992. The site of Paul's Texaco (right), which was on the west side of Seventy-seventh Court, at 7733 Belmont Avenue, is today home to the Mason Plaza Condominiums, built in 1978.

The empty lots at the Northwest corner of Elmwood Park was often the site of a temporary ice rink, where the north side children would ice-skate in the days before the apartment buildings fronted Belmont Avenue. This view is looking southeast from Pacific and Belmont Avenues. Note the wires above the street, which were used for the trolley buses. Trolley buses were electric buses that ran in Chicago until 1973.

This is none other than NFL Hall of Famer Ray Nitschke, on the football field at Proviso. The smile on his face hides a rough childhood. Ray was only three years old, living at 2547 North Seventy-fifth Court, when his father was killed in an automobile accident. His mother died a few years later. The corner of Seventy-sixth and Diversey Avenues was named in Nitschke's honor. Other sports legends that have lived in the village include Ron Santo, who played for both the White Sox and the Cubs, and former Blackhawk Jerry "King Kong" Korab. (Author's collection.)

Four

MANGIA!

Mangia means "Eat!" in Italian, and Elmwood Park has always been a place where a person could get a great meal at a decent price. This tradition started way back on George Marwood's farm with the first village picnic and continues today with the annual Taste of Elmwood Park.

It would be impossible to list all of the great places to eat that have existed since the village began. Some of the earliest were the Thatcher Inn at North and Thatcher Avenues and Hayes at North and Harlem Avenues.

From sandwiches served at taverns to full-blown banquet halls, Elmwood Park has seen them all. A stretch of North Avenue from what was once Nielsen's Village down to Johnnie's Beef is known as Restaurant Row. The New Star Restaurant has been serving up Cantonese food there since 1954. Other longtime village favorites include Jim & Pete's, Massa, Trattoria Peppino, and several others offering everything from Cuban delicacies to sushi. Along with the restaurants there have been dozens of small neighborhood delis, bakeries, and even long-standing grocery stores like Caputo's and Buy-Wise (now known as Super-Low Foods).

Generations made their way to Claudio Pastry for some cannoli siciliane, or Gene's Delicatessen on Harlem Avenue for a submarine sandwich. Other favorite stops included the Kentucky Fried Chicken at 7530 Grand Avenue, which became Harpo's Grand Dogs, then the Dog House, and is now a Baci pizza. There was Chicken Unlimited on Belmont Avenue and a Peter Pan on Harlem Avenue.

These gastronomic delights are spread all over the village, from Restaurant Row to the Elmwood Family restaurant on Belmont Avenue, and from Wingstop on Harlem Avenue to Russell's on Thatcher Avenue. At the Circle was the Jewel, which became a White Hen and is now a convenience store. There was also the Maple Tree Pancake House down the street from what is now Baciami Restaurant. It is impossible to list all of the eateries, but the following pages are sure to stir up an appetite or at the very least some memories.

The village picnic of 1915 was held on George Marwood's farm at Beach and Armitage Avenues. Among those enjoying the open-pit barbecue were George Marwood, Ed Peters, Sam Arado, Walter Schumacher, and Louis Longfield. Ardo was the first person to apply for an Elmwood Park building permit when he built a tavern at 7200 West Grand Avenue.

The intersection of North and Thatcher Avenues has always been the quietest entrance into the village. In the 1930s, the Thatcher Inn was located on the northeast corner. It was a casual establishment where diners could fill their bellies, along with their gas tanks. The owners were taken for $146 in a 1939 robbery. That seemingly meager sum is equal to about $2,400 today.

Hayes Restaurant was a longtime fixture on the northwest corner of Harlem and North Avenues. What had started as a barbecue stand evolved into a fine restaurant. It is mentioned by name, along with Nielsen's Restaurant, in Father Andrew Greely's novel *Younger Than Springtime*. The building was demolished in 1954, and the location has been home to a Walgreens for many years.

In 1935, Erickson's Tavern was touted as Elmwood Park's oldest tavern. Located at 7353 Grand Avenue, it was known to have the finest dance floor and was praised for Mrs. Erickson's famous chicken sandwiches, served with coleslaw for only a quarter. Al Blodgett is the friendly bartender seen here, ready to serve up a cold brew.

* FREE PARKING * NO COVER * NO MINIMUM *

FIRST NAME BAND NOW AT THE SKY CLUB

OPENING THURSDAY
MARCH 21
ANSON WEEKS
and
HIS ORCHESTRA

DANCING NIGHTLY
DELICIOUS DINNERS
SPECIAL ARRANGE-
MENTS FOR PARTIES
AND BANQUETS

Private Dining Room Available

MENU

Half Roast Chicken......$1.75
Chicken Fricassee $1.75
Prime Roast of Beef,
  Au jus Sauce.......$1.50
Roast Loin of Pork,
  Apple Sauce
Pepper Steak, Mushrooms..$1.50
Roast Leg o' Lamb with
  Mint Sauce
Fried Liver and Bacon....$1.50
French Grilled Lamb
  Chops (2 Lamb Chops) $1.75
Top Sirloin Butt Steak....$1.50
Filet Mignon, Mushrooms $2.00
Broiled Whitefish
French Fried Frog Legs....$1.65
Choice Sirloin Steak......$1.50
Price of Dinner includes choice
  of Appetizer, Soup, Salad, Po-
  tatoes, Vegetable, Dessert and
  Beverage.

"Dancin' with Anson"

LARRY CONTI
AND HIS
11-PC. ORCHESTRA
DANCING NIGHTLY

FOR
RESERVATIONS
ELMwood Park
RIVer Grove 2893

Sky CLUB
HARLEM AND NORTH

The featured act in this 1940s Sky Club advertisement is a band led by Anson Weeks. Bing Crosby's brother Bob had once been the vocalist for the popular West Coast dance band. In the 1950s, the club featured Cirene, "the Aqua Queen," who danced underwater. Appropriately enough, the club advertised itself as "a place where the air swims with music."

This unidentified couple is enjoying a night out at Elmwood Park's swankiest nightclub in 1944. The Sky Club, at 1630 North Harlem Avenue, was popular with servicemen home from the war and those about to head overseas. It remained popular well into the 1950s. In the years prior to its closing, the Sky Club occasionally featured all-girl revues and was reputed to host gambling.

OLSON'S *Chicago's*

Finest RESTAURANT

7330 W. NORTH AVENUE
RIVER GROVE 1394

"Look for the Rustic Fence"

Olson's Restaurant was one of the early establishments on what would later be known as Restaurant Row. Built in 1936 at 7330 West North Avenue, the restaurant with "the rustic fence" would later become Nielsen's. After Nielsen's closed, the building was demolished and a Total Beverage was opened, which is now a Binny's Beverage Depot. Note the River Grove telephone exchange.

The sprawling Nielsen's restaurant was in its heyday at the time this postcard was printed. Danish immigrant Aksel Nielsen opened the business in the mid-1940s. It featured a traditional smorgasbord and served meals on black-and-pink-trimmed plates. The longtime North Avenue landmark also featured a popular banquet hall. (Author's collection.)

Russell's Bar-B-Q, a local landmark at 1621 Thatcher Avenue, has been delighting patrons for many years. The unique structure, with its classic wooden booths, had a rough beginning. The original building on that site was destroyed by fire in April 1949. In 1950, the current building's first year, a bombing and two fires took place. One blaze cost the watchman his life. The case remains unsolved as of 2013.

Even though the restaurant is slightly off the beaten path, generations have flocked to Russell's after baseball or soccer games, a day spent at Kiddieland, or before or after catching a movie at the Mercury Theatre. People continue to enjoy the classic recipes today and eat in the same booths where their parents or grandparents dined.

This 1951 advertisement for Horwath's touts "hospitality and good food." Horwath's was also known as a place where some of Chicago's crime bosses would gather to meet and eat. Law enforcement officials were known to stake out the parking lot and watch the customers come and go. It was here that Charles "Chuckie" English met his end when he was shot and killed in a 1985 unsolved murder.

HOSPITALITY AND GOOD FOOD

When you dine out you want to enjoy yourself—and that means you want not only excellent food, but efficient service and pleasant atmosphere. You'll enjoy them here at Horwath's—for your all around dining satisfaction. Stop in tonight!

(4-21-51)

HORWATH'S RESTAURANT
1850 N. HARLEM
Phone GLadstone 3-0413

The classic Horwath's sign and a linden tree decorated with lights were landmarks along Harlem Avenue. Horwath's welcomed diners for decades. A trust bought the property in 2002 and closed the restaurant. The building's swan song was a television appearance, in an episode of *The West Wing*, prior to demolition. A Staples office supply store is now located on the site.

In 1929, Alberto Biancalana opened an ice cream parlor at 7372 Grand Avenue, which he then turned into a restaurant/pizza parlor named Al's Place. As the eatery's clientele continued to grow, the name was changed to Biancalana's. The business, still owned by the family, is now known as Elmcrest Banquets by Biancalana.

In 1974, when this photograph was taken, one could walk into Stammer's Market, also home to Donz Bakery, 7628–30 North Avenue, and purchase a famous pound cake or an all-butter coffee cake. The owners of the market, Charles and Bess Stammer, ran the business there for many years. The building has housed Larrabee Herbs since 1999.

The Caira family has owned the Cities Service gas station, at 7835 Belmont Avenue, since 1962. Three generations have been repairing autos at the location now known as Caira Super Service. In the 1960s, the shop was sandwiched between the Owl Snack shop (left) and a Chicken Unlimited at 7837 Belmont Avenue. The Owl Snack shop building at 7821 Belmont Avenue later housed a Century 21 office and is currently home to TitleMax.

Little has changed at Johnnie's Beef since William Hartney took this photograph in 1974. The menu still features its famous beef, sausage, or combo sandwiches, dry or juicy, with or without peppers. A meal at Johnnie's often includes Italian lemonade, also called an ice. Long lines form year-round, but especially on hot summer days and nights. Johnnie's opened in 1961 in the uniquely shaped building that had housed a hotdog stand.

Armand's Restaurant, seen in this 1970s collage, opened in 1956 in the former Victory Tap building at 7404 Grand Avenue. The restaurant, renowned for its stuffed artichokes and thin-crust pizza, closed in 2009. The Caringella family decided to franchise the name and recipes, and, in 2010, those delicacies once again became available at Armand's Pizzeria Express, at 7650 North Avenue. (Author's collection.)

Angelo and Romana Caputo opened their New Farm Produce & Italian Specialties store at Harlem and Wrightwood Avenues in 1958. In the beginning, Angelo would travel daily to the South Water Market in the wee hours of the morning to buy the freshest fruits and produce he could find and sell them later that day in his store. The store was expanded many times after this photograph was taken in 1972.

There were several small restaurant/lounges located within the village. There was Al & Mary's Lounge at 7298 Diversey Avenue, Jurek's at 7327 West Fullerton Avenue, and Bambi's, located on Seventy-fourth Avenue, to name a few. Here, the photographer is facing south toward Diversey Avenue in 1976. There was a small gas station on the corner. Both buildings are now gone, and the lot is empty. The family-run business lent its name to the park located just north on Seventy-fourth Avenue.

Luigi and Anna Maria Barbi opened the Alpine Food Shop at 7538 North Avenue and ran the business for 45 years. The small neighborhood deli is renowned for its sandwiches. In 2000, the Bonaccorsi brothers purchased the business and have continued to run it much as it was when this photograph was taken in 1974.

The Whistle Stop Restaurant was torn down in 1971 and replaced by Gas City. The charming roadside diner paid homage to the ever-present trains that ran on the tracks behind 7750 Grand Avenue with its very own locomotive, perched atop the depot-styled outdoor seating area. A Phillips 66 now occupies the site.

In the 1960s, the Albano Bakery at 7816 North Avenue was one of several Italian bakeries in the Elmwood Park area. Locals would often walk to their favorite bakery to buy their cuccidati (Italian fig cookies), cannoli, and zeppoli, along with cakes and other sweets once made by white-haired grandmothers. The building is now home to Bernard A. Affetto & Co., certified public accountants.

It is hard to imagine that the small independent convenience store at 22 Conti Parkway was once a Jewel Tea Company store. The precursor to today's Jewel Osco's was once a simple neighborhood market. The store was remodeled and enlarged in 1958 and eventually became a White Hen Pantry. Wonder Woman was even scheduled to make a live appearance at the White Hen on June 29, 1976.

The Taste of Elmwood Park began in 1985 and was modeled after the St. Celestine annual cookouts. The fest was originally held on the Fourth of July weekend in the Circle, but it was relocated to Central Park when the aquatic center was built. It was also held at the high school, but took place at Central Park once again in 2013. The event was organized by the civic foundation under the leadership of Al Biancalana. On a sad note, longtime emcee Mr. Fourth of July, Ernie Vessini, unexpectedly passed away on his beloved holiday in 2000.

When Sally's Beauty Supply moved across Harlem Avenue, it gave Caputo's a chance for another much-needed expansion. The remodeling doubled the establishment's size and included an overhaul of the facade. On February 16, 2010, the Caputo family opened a new flagship store at Harlem and Grand Avenues. The old building, seen here in 2003, has become a Planet Fitness health club.

Several of the area's most prominent politicians ham it up at the 1957 Leyden Municipal League Picnic with a mock eating competition. Shown here are, from left to right, (first row) Rosemont mayor Donald Stephens, River Grove mayor Richard J. O'Connor, and Elmwood Park president Elmer Conti; (second row) Leyden supervisor Adolph J. Bochte, municipal judge Alvin J. Kvistad, and Schiller Park mayor Ed Bluthardt.

Five

THE CONTI YEARS

Between 1914 and 1953, Elmwood Park had 10 presidents. The longest-serving president, John Cullerton, held the office for 13 years, from 1935 until 1948. These relatively short terms, averaging about four years, changed when Elmer Conti came onto the scene. Elmer was the first village president to be born and raised in Elmwood Park. Prior to being elected to the top position, he served four years as a village trustee. Conti became the only president a generation would know, holding the office for 32 years.

Conti attended Proviso High School, where he was a gifted athlete. In fact, he played two seasons with the Chicago Cardinals professional football team. In addition to his job leading the village, Conti served three terms in the Illinois General Assembly. During his tenure, the village would build a giant water reservoir, a new high school, a post office, a library, and a civic center. He led the village during the civil rights movement and the beginning of the Cold War. Some would thank him, and others would curse him, for the decision to build within the Circle. In 1960, Conti proposed forming a town called the Village of Leyden, which would have been composed of Elmwood Park, River Grove, Franklin Park, Schiller Park, and the Township of Leyden, as a means to oppose further annexations by Chicago and to consolidate costs among the villages.

Conti was always looking at the big picture. He was rewarded for his accomplishments when Elmwood Parkway was renamed Conti Parkway. The Conti years were in some ways a time of innocence, when people left their doors unlocked, knew all their neighbors, and felt a community spirit. That spirit would come to life during the golden jubilee. Hopefully, the following photographs will rekindle the feelings of the time.

Elmer Conti was the longest-serving president in the village's history. Born and raised in Elmwood Park, he served as president for 32 years, from 1953 to 1985. He was president of the Leyden Savings & Loan Association, was a Leyden Township Republican committeeman for 27 years, and drafted 118 bills that became laws as a member of the Illinois General Assembly (1956–1962).

Located in River Forest, St. Vincent Ferrer, shown here in the winter of 1979, was organized in 1922 to serve the north side of River Forest and the southern half of Elmwood Park. The first church was a small frame structure facing North Avenue. In 1940, a school was built. On June 29, 1954, ground was broken for the present church, consecrated on September 23, 1956.

What at first glance appears to be a steel teepee or oil well is actually Elmwood Park's landmark water tower as it appeared during construction in 1954. The tower was the epicenter of the $900,000 water system, which was needed as the village population jumped from 13,500 in 1940 to 21,517 just 14 years later.

The installation of Elmwood Park's water tower in 1954 was the crowning moment in the modernization of the village's water supply. The tower holds only 250,000 gallons, with the belowground reservoir holding an additional two million gallons. The overhead tank helped boost the water pressure, from five pounds or less in parts of the village, to a uniform 45 pounds. A playground was built atop the reservoir.

In the early 1950s, the communities that had been taking in Elmwood Park high school students began to bar entry to their schools. Oak Park River Forest was the only school that would accept freshmen in 1952. In 1954, Elmwood Park sought a solution by establishing its own high school district. A school was built on land that once belonged to the Oak Park Country Club. Other locations had been proposed, including the Holy Cross site and Evans Field.

Like a scene straight out of *Happy Days* or *Grease*, bobby-soxers and greasers make up the student body roaming the halls of Elmwood Park High School in 1959. The wide hallways and spacious layout had been a welcome change over the portable buildings that initially served as the high school. The four-year high school, at 8201 West Fullerton Avenue, received rave reviews when its doors opened in 1955.

Elmwood Park High School fielded its first football team in 1954. The team, called the Tigers, has since dropped the all-white uniforms and now wears black and gold. In 2012, the team won the Metro Suburban Conference title for the first time since 1985. In 2005, a synthetic-grass, all-weather field replaced the natural grass. This has resulted in a dramatic improvement in playing conditions. (Courtesy of Elmwood Park High School.)

Majestic vase-shaped American elm trees once lined many of the streets, such as the section of Westwood Avenue seen in this Charles Schonert photograph. Dutch elm disease reached the Chicago area in 1954, causing the original trees to be cut down and replaced by other species. In 2013, the emerald ash borer is destroying the replacement ash trees, many of which may meet a similar fate.

In the days before big-box stores such as Lowes and Home Depot, smaller, independent home-improvement centers flourished. One survivor is Beacon Home Improvement Center, which has been located at 7719 Belmont Avenue since the 1950s. The business continues today as Beacon Kitchen & Bath, Inc., with an updated facade.

The L. Fish Furniture Company opened its 10th store, at 7205 Grand Avenue, on February 25, 1954. The building was once home to a Montgomery Ward store, which left for a larger building. The business, founded in 1859, was named after founder David Fish's wife, Lotta. The building, which was demolished after a fire, stood at the site of the parking lot now used by the Italo-American Maroons Club, which occupies the building that housed the Grand Hardware store (right).

First Security Trust and Savings Bank had previously been the First State Bank. The institution changed its name when it moved to a new building at 7315 Grand Avenue. Arthur M. Wirtz owner of the Chicago Blackhawks was the principal owner of the bank. The Stanley Cup visited the bank after the Blackhawks won the championship in 1961 and 2010. The cup paid another visit on September 8, 2013, in celebration of the Blackhawks' 2013 National Hockey League championship.

The fire department employed this customized 1956 Ford country sedan as a foam unit. Foam is used to fight liquid fires, floating on the surface and smothering the fire rather than spreading it. The large number of tanker cars riding the rails through town made this unique piece of equipment a necessity in the event of a derailment.

The businesses surrounding the Circle have changed over the years, and few have had the staying power of Cutler's Drugs. For 40 years, Isadore Cutler ran a pharmacy in the Circle. He was one of several independent pharmacists in the village. Cutler's Drugs was located at 20 Conti Parkway until he moved a few doors down to No. 16. The old site eventually became the Maple Tree Pancake House.

The Elmwood Park police, seen here in 1961, have kept a watchful eye over the village. A few years before this photograph was taken, in the early morning of November 4, 1957, their watch included the sky. On that date, at 3:12 a.m., patrolmen Joseph Lukasek and Clifford Schau and fireman Robert Volz spotted a UFO over the Elmwood Cemetery and chased it for one and a half miles. Officer Dan DiGiovanni, among others, also saw it. The well-documented event was even featured on a television special.

The third edifice to house the public library was at 7705 Westwood Drive. In May 1939, a lease was signed for the vacant storefront that the library would call home for the next 36 years. Although the building was remodeled and enlarged in 1962, the need for an even larger facility was apparent. The building was later demolished after the library made its controversial move to the interior of the Circle.

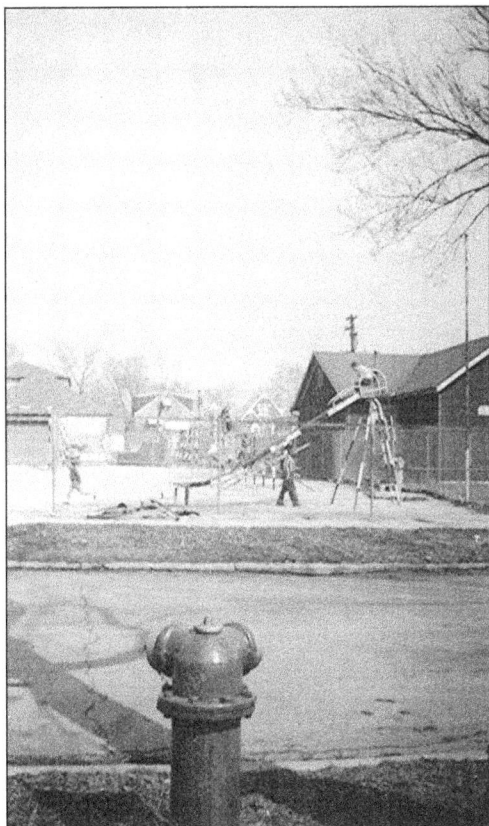

Bambi Park on Seventy-fourth Avenue, just north of Diversey Avenue, is seen here around 1948. The building on the right was the American Legion hall, which had been an old portable school in the 1920s. The school district sold the 200-foot-by-125-foot lot at 2821 North Seventy-fourth Avenue to the village in 1961. The building, called "a frame shack" by village manager Howard Olsen, was demolished in 1962.

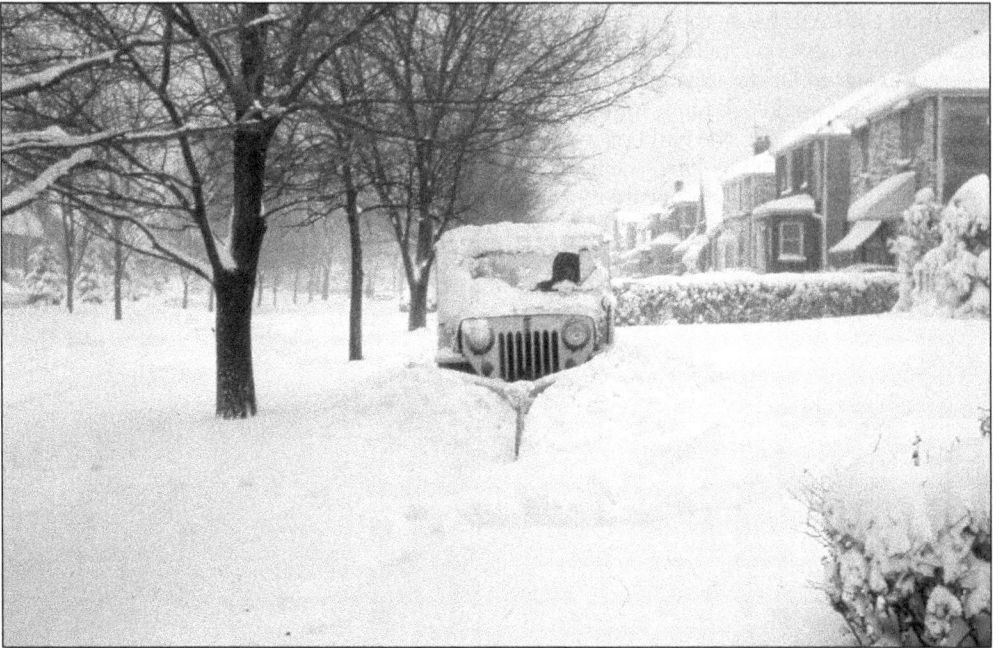

On Groundhog Day, February 2, 2011, a snowfall measuring 21.2 inches blanketed the area, stranding motorists and residents alike. It was the third-biggest snowstorm in the history of the area. Those who have lived here since the early 1960s may remember a time when the village used this Jeep to clear the sidewalks after big storms.

The top of the village's two-million-gallon reservoir was designed to house recreational facilities, including a playground, tennis courts, and basketball courts. In 1962, ice-skating and hockey were added to that list. In the background can be seen Grand Harlem Motors, 7329 Grand Avenue, and the Goldblatts water tower.

The Berlin airlift and Cuban missile crisis were two events that made the possibility of a nuclear war seem very real. As a result, there was much interest in fallout shelters to protect families from radiation. Here, a civil defense demonstration is held in front of Vince's Cleaners in the Circle. There is no telling how many residents actually installed a shelter in their yards, but those that did eventually turned them into expensive storage spaces.

People featured on National Geographic Channel's *Doomsday Preppers* have nothing on Harold Eckardt's fallout shelter, seen here in the early 1960s in the basement of his home at 2047 North Seventy-fourth Avenue. Eckardt won a Home Preparedness award for his well-stocked basement. In addition to essential items such as food and water, he kept hand tools, candles, and flashlights at the ready.

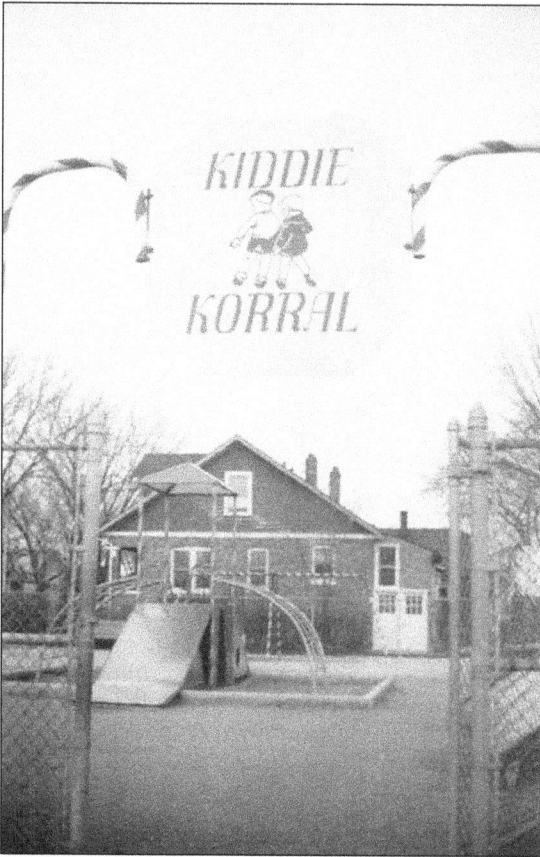

The Kiddie Korral, shown here in 1961, is located at Seventy-fifth Court and Dickens Avenue. It was one of just a few playgrounds and green spaces located on the south side of the village. In fact, prior to the opening of Centennial Park, it was the only public park between Fullerton and North Avenues. The park was renovated in 1998.

Bicycle parades, in which children decorate their bikes with crepe paper, balloons, and other adornments, are a long-standing tradition in the village. The children are given a chance to show off their creativity. This 1960s parade featured a young man who takes it to the next level with his *carrettu siciliano*. His colorful Sicilian-styled "cart" even came equipped with a donkey.

In 1961, the Women's Club started a fund to restore the Circle's neglected and vandalized fountain. They pledged to split the cost of the restoration with the village, and they raised $1,500. The club purchased several statues for the top of the fountain to replace those that had been stolen or broken. The fountain was later sold to a private developer when the Mills family relinquished control of the Circle park.

This photograph shows trees being planted between Eastbrook and Westbrook Avenues. The streets are a visible reminder of the creek that at one time ran along Eightieth Avenue, through what is the Oak Park Country Club, and eventually into the Des Plaines River. The creek is probably responsible for the occasional flooding that continues to plague the area.

The Grover D. Rose Stadium was located at 8200 West Belmont, which is actually in River Grove. At that time, the area bounded by what is now O'Connor Drive north to Belmont Avenue and from Cumberland Avenue to 80th Avenue was vacant land and unused Elmwood Cemetery property until Holy Cross High School was built in the early 1960s. Grover Rose was the president of the Elmwood Cemetery.

Judging by the array of helmets, this pickup football game, in the Circle park, took place in the early 1960s. In the background is the Circle 5 and 10 store. The business, owned by Maurice Kirts from 1947 until 1971 and later by his son, was known for creaky wooden floors and a mechanical horse. The horse now resides in the library, and the building now houses Baciami restaurant.

The Grand Harlem Coal Company was one of the few industrial operations located within the village. Access to the rail lines next to 7300 Fullerton Avenue made the site attractive to the company, once known as Hagemann's Coal Yard. The residential switch from coal to natural gas was ultimately the demise of the company. The building was demolished to make room for the post office, which now occupies the site.

Elmwood Park finally got its own post office in 1963. Seen here during construction in 1962, the building was officially dedicated on August 31, 1963. It was constructed on the site of the old coal yard at 7300 West Fullerton Avenue (see previous caption). The 10,000-square-foot building employed 79 carriers and personnel. It continues to serve the village today.

Triangle Park is another of the small neighborhood playgrounds located throughout the village. The aptly named park is located on a parcel of land bordered by Diversey Avenue to the north, Seventy-seventh Avenue on the east, and Elmgrove Drive on the west. In this 1964 photograph, the slide seems to be the most popular attraction, while a group of teeter-totters stands at the ready.

This US Army M3 Stuart tank served as Elmwood Park's war memorial from 1947 until 1998, when it was taken to the Kenosha Military Museum. Originally located at Grand Avenue and Sunset Drive, the tank was moved into the Circle in the 1970s, when Grand Avenue was widened. The tank replaced an earlier war memorial, a World War I artillery gun, which was scrapped during World War II. Ironically, an artillery gun replaced the tank in 1999.

Some of Elmwood Park's loveliest young ladies were chosen at a pageant to represent the village during the golden jubilee as the queen and her court. Shown here are, from left to right, (first row) Linda Chum, Diane Mattaresse, and Marilyn Haislet; (second row) Janice Kaska, Mary Litrenta, and Carol Ann Rogers. Seated at the top is Queen Audrey Larson.

The crowd that came out to view the golden jubilee parade on September 7, 1964, was as interesting and colorful as the parade itself. This festive group chose to gather at the war memorial, located at the meeting point of Sunset Drive, Seventy-sixth Avenue, and Grand Avenue. A couple of boys even grabbed the coveted spot atop the tank.

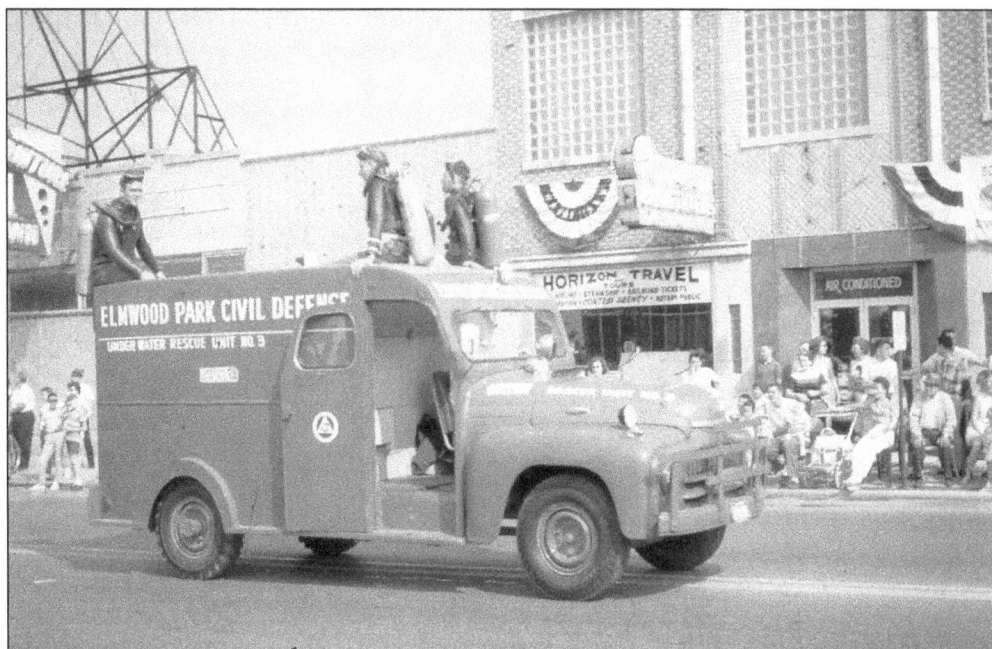

The Elmwood Park Civil Defense was prepared for any sort of emergency, from a nuclear attack to a plane or train crash. Civil Defense director Ossie Hjellum, of 2835 Seventy-second Court, preferred to call it "disaster defense." Even though the village is a noncoastal community, the proximity of the Des Plaines River created the potential for an underwater rescue.

As part of the golden jubilee, the celebration committee staged a dramatic production entitled *Prairie to Prosperity*. The full-scale ensemble, which included live horses, was a 15-scene reenactment of the village's history and featured a cast of over 100 residents. Shown here is scene 4, "The New Land."

Baseball has always been popular in the village, and this field served as the home for many local teams. The field, located at what is now Guerin Prep High School, just south of Belmont Avenue and west of Eightieth Avenue, was constructed almost entirely by the fathers of the players. The Playroom, at 7958 Belmont Avenue, can be seen just beyond left-center field.

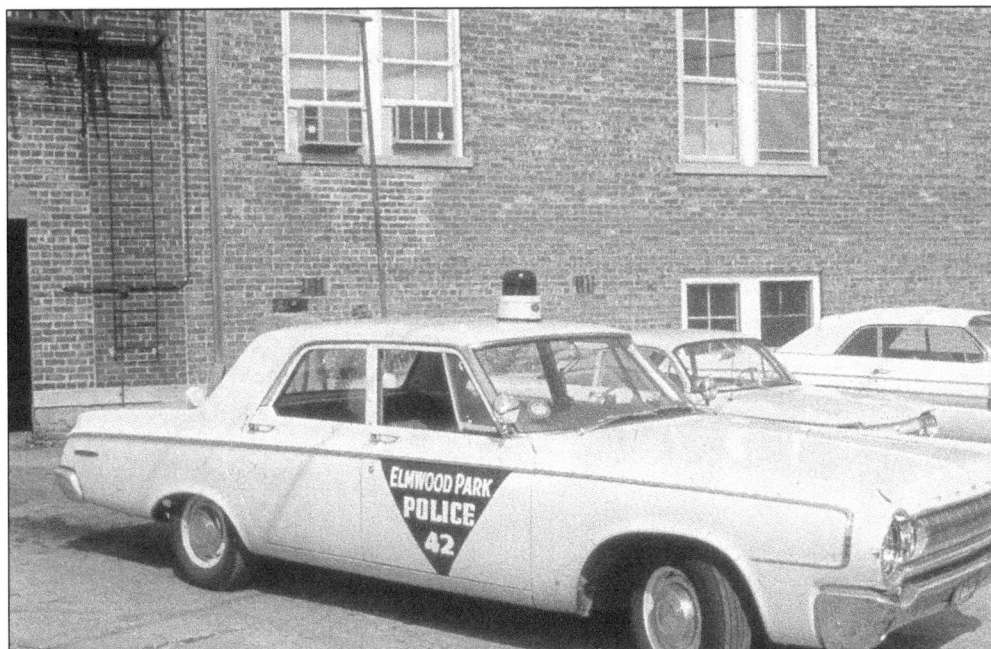

People who grew up in the village in the 1960s often refer to a Mayberry-like existence. Perhaps contributing to those reminiscences are images of the era's police cars. The white police car with the single bubblegum light, seen here in 1964, does resemble the black-and-white car Sheriff Andy Taylor drives in the fictional small town on *The Andy Griffith Show*.

In 1941, the North Side Gospel Center acquired a small brick church built by the Elmwood Park Free Methodists on Seventy-fifth Avenue just south of Fullerton Avenue, reopening it as the Elmwood Park Gospel Center. In 1964, construction began on a new church, and the name was changed to the Elmwood Park Bible Church. On Good Friday 1966, the old church was razed. It was replaced by the parking lot there today and seen in the foreground.

A well-remembered annual event was the water fights that took place between fire departments on the Fourth of July. A barrel was attached to a cable suspended several feet above ground. Fire crews would adjust the spray from their hoses to push the barrel until it reached a certain spot on the wire. The refreshing spray would cool those gathered to view the battle.

In fine Chicago tradition, a chair is ready to serve as a placeholder when this young man finally digs a car out from under the record 23-inch snowfall of January 26–27, 1967. This scene took place on the 3100 block of Seventy-seventh Court, but it was a sight witnessed throughout the community over the several days it took residents to dig out. Amazingly, the temperature had hit 65 degrees just two days earlier.

When the fire department first strung Christmas lights on the water tower, it began a tradition that has continued for well over 40 years. A well-timed snowfall adds to the festive nature of this photograph, which was taken of the Fullerton Avenue firehouse in 1970. For many years, John Litrenta Jr. had the perilous task of stringing the lights.

When the current St. Celestine's Church building was constructed in the late 1960s and early 1970s, it was built on the site of the parking lot. This created a need for a new parking lot, which was created by demolishing a home and moving a few others that were located directly north of the old church. Adm. Hyman G. Rickover, "Father of the Nuclear Navy," was married in the new church in a private, "top secret" service in 1974. (Courtesy of St. Celestine's.)

This aerial photograph shows the old and new St. Celestine's Churches alongside one another. The new church was vastly different from the initial design, proposed in 1959. The first plans were traditional in style, with a large tower alongside the building. The Vatican II Council dictated a more modern design, stressing a communal feeling and warmth, over the old cathedral styles. The older church was demolished in the mid-1970s and replaced with the pastoral center. (Courtesy of St. Celestine's.)

The Circle Park was a serene and shaded oasis that held all types of events, from July 4th celebrations and concerts to art fairs like the one seen here. The large open space was a welcome reprieve from the hustle and bustle of the city, which was literally within walking distance of the Circle, yet seemed so much farther.

The electrical department helped with tree removal from the late 1950s through the early 1970s. Dutch elm disease decimated the town's namesake tree species, and many previously tree-lined streets were laid bare. The mature elm trees had produced a cathedral-like effect, as the vase-shaped trees on either side of the street touched each other. The disease reached its peak in 1970, when 600 trees were cut down.

The north section of the Circle provided the perfect setting for an afternoon skate in the winter of 1972. A year later, the heirs of John Mills agreed to the building of the civic center in the Circle. The library, which came later, was built on the site of the rink. In the background can be seen the First Church of Christ, Scientist, which was instituted in 1950 at 32 Elmwood Parkway.

Perhaps no issue in the village's history was as hotly debated as development in the Circle. This parade float from 1972 was built by those opposed to developing the park, which John Mills had donated to the village with the intent of keeping it open space. Mills's heirs agreed to the plans for the civic center the following year. A pool was installed several years later.

This castle-like structure in this postcard montage was known as Ye Olde Leather Bottle Pub. Located at 7353 West Grand Avenue, it was famous for its pan pizza. Formerly the Twist Lounge, it was the scene of a 1972 killing of a convicted arsonist that could have been the plot of a television movie. The suspects were described as "two sexy blondes." The building was leveled in 1980 by the Biancalanas to create additional parking. (Author's collection.)

The former Elm Theatre was reincarnated as Armanetti's Liquors in the late 1960s. The grand entrance and several storefronts were removed to provide additional parking. In later years, the structure became home to Westwood True Value Hardware, which closed in 2006. The main auditorium, still standing, is currently vacant.

The Jehovah's Witnesses formed an Elmwood Park congregation in 1940. They built the Kingdom Hall at 7309 Fullerton Avenue in a time when open fields and single-family homes surrounded it. A Kingdom Hall is different from a church in that it is devoid of religious emblems and fixtures, but serves as an auditorium for religious study and lectures.

Cameo Towers, seen here in 1972, was the first skyscraper to be built in Elmwood Park. Construction of the 19-story building at 7234 North Avenue was approved in 1965 after a seven-month court battle. The mixed-use building features commercial units and 176 residential units and amenities such as a 19th-floor penthouse party room and a fifth-floor outdoor pool. The building was converted to condominiums in 1978.

On September 9, 1974, a group of residents and members of the library board joined village president Elmer Conti (left of center) for the ground breaking of the new library in the Circle. Among those present that day was the village historian, Edwin Emmerling (far left).

On October 6, 1975, the doors opened on the 14,700-square-foot public library at 4 Conti Parkway, inside of the Circle. The new building was part of the controversial development of the Circle park that began with the building of the civic center. The building became the Early Childhood Center after the current library was constructed in 2002.

The original entrance to the Elmwood Park High School auditorium/gymnasium is seen here in 1972. The photograph predates the library addition, built in 1975–1976. The addition was part of a system-wide renovation plan for the schools. The high school, which was built for 1,000 students, had an enrollment of 1,200 in 1971 and was expecting more students in coming years.

The Royal Elm Geriatric Center was built in 1973–1974 on the former site of the Westwood Laundry. When completed, the 24-hour care facility claimed to be the only nursing home equipped with a "complete sprinkler system." In 2010, the four-story, 245-bed facility, now called Elmwood Care, was remodeled. It now includes an ice cream parlor and flat-screen televisions.

Service Chevrolet, located at 2828 North Harlem Avenue, had a long run in the village. Located on Grand Avenue in the 1950s, the dealership thrived at the Harlem Avenue address through the 1960s and 1970s. Ultimately, the dealer went bankrupt, and a Handy Andy home improvement center took over the site, which now is home to Walgreens.

In May 1976, residents braved the weather to catch a glimpse of the motorcade of Queen Margrethe II of Denmark as it drove through the Circle. The queen visited the Elmwood Park Press, which was home to the *Danish Pioneer*, one of only two Danish-language newspapers in the country at that time. The paper, which began in 1872, was published in Elmwood Park from 1958 until 1984.

Halloween's popularity as a holiday has been growing over the years, with people throwing elaborate parties. But many folks are just as satisfied with old-fashioned candy collecting. The ghosts and goblins roaming Elmwood Park streets on Halloween in 1976 had a pleasant day to gather their treats. A dry day with temperatures in the mid-50s was perfect weather for trick-or-treating, as this unidentified group could attest.

The "knife sharpener guy's" bell would announce his approach as he traveled the sidewalks of the village. He would sharpen anything, from knives and shears to scissors, much to the delight of the housewives and the children who watched as he honed blades on his foot-pedal grinding wheels. A nearly mythological figure today, such tradesmen are rarely seen, pushing their carts, much like this one in the 1970s.

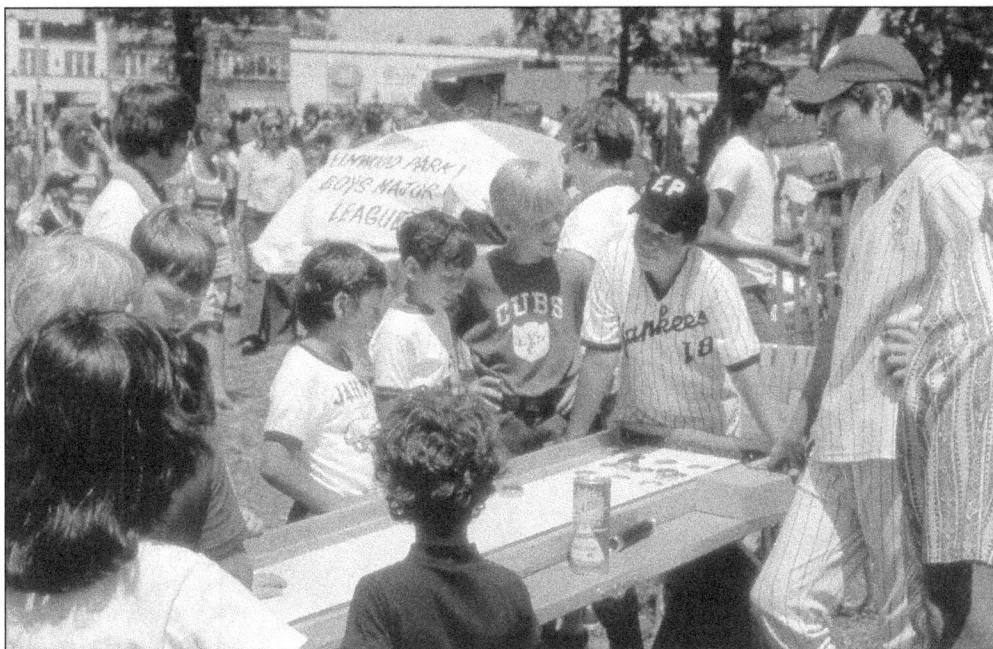

This image of the Circle was taken in July 1978. By all accounts, it is probably the Fourth of July. Some would say that scenes like this inspired former Elmwood Park resident and founding member of the band Chicago, trumpeter Lee Loughnane. Perhaps his memories had some influence on bandmate Robert Lamm, who penned one of the band's biggest hits, "Saturday in the Park."

In 1977, George Randazzo founded the National Italian-American Sports Hall of Fame. Its first location was in this union hall at 7906 Grand Avenue, which is currently home to Michael's Uniform. Originally, the hall focused on boxers, but soon added all sports. In 1988, it moved to Arlington Heights. The hall moved again in 2000 into a new facility at 1431 West Taylor Street in Chicago.

The current neighbors of 2531 North Seventy-sixth Avenue would probably be interested in knowing that what appears to be a normal single-family home was once the only hospital in the village. During the 1920s, the house, once owned by a Dr. Eastman, served in that capacity, probably due to its proximity to the center of town.

On July 4, 1980, Frank Vesper snapped this photograph at the dedication of the Peace Monument in front of the municipal building. Structures of note in the photograph are the apartment building where the library now stands, the Union 76 gas station where the firehouse is today, and the Fotomat kiosk. Fotomats were drive-up overnight film-development kiosks. They became obsolete in the late 1980s as one-hour photo development became commonplace.

Six

THE SILVESTRI ERA

With Elmer Conti's decision not run again for village president in 1985, an era came to an end. Then, after Don Storino's and Richard Torpe's brief terms in office, a new face arrived on the political stage, another longtime resident of the village named Peter Silvestri.

Silvestri, who began his career in public service on the school board, was appointed a village trustee in 1988. In 1989, Silvestri was elected village president, a position he would hold for 24 years. His passion for public service was recognized with the naming of the Peter N. Silvestri Cultural and Learning Center at the Elmwood Park Library.

Increasing green space, expanding recreational areas, and upgrading outdated village facilities and services were among Silvestri's top priorities. During his time in office, several large projects came to fruition, including a recreation center addition, the creation of Central Park, Centennial Park, John Mills Park, Torpe Park, and a new skate park and rink on Fullerton Avenue, along with upgrades to the existing village playgrounds. A new public safety building replaced the old south fire station. Computers were added to the police cars, and a reverse 911 system was installed to alert residents of potential emergencies.

There have also been changes to the business districts. Some familiar names left the scene, like Nielsen's and Horwath's, and new businesses took their places. New shopping plazas appeared at Seventy-second Court and North Avenue, at Harlem and Wabansia Avenues, and at Diversey and Harlem Avenues. The Grand and Harlem Avenue area was recently spruced up, with a new gateway fountain. Soon, new development will be occurring on the south side of Grand Avenue. The community is also more culturally and ethnically diverse than it has ever been.

The Silvestri era was a time of continued growth and change. As that period ends, a new era is beginning as Angelo "Skip" Saviano assumes the big chair. What will the next 100 years bring? Will the flood mitigation project finally solve the flooding issues? Will an overpass or underpass for the railroad ever be built? It remains to be seen, but one thing is sure: the next 100 years should be as interesting as the first.

Peter Silvestri started his political career as a school board member. He was appointed to the position of village trustee in 1988. In 1989, he ran a successful campaign for the village presidency, a position he would hold for the next 24 years. Silvestri has also served the community as the Cook County commissioner for the ninth district since 1994. (Courtesy of the Village of Elmwood Park.)

In 1988, Vice Pres. George H.W. Bush visited Elmwood Park while campaigning for president. His trip coincided with the annual Taste of Elmwood Park. Here, he shares the stage with, from left to right, Donald E. Stephens, Sheriff Jim O'Grady, Peter Silvestri, Al Biancalana, Barbara Bush, acting village president Richard Torpe, and Skip Saviano. At lower left, ever-vigilant police chief Dewey Paoletti keeps a watchful eye on the crowd.

Elmwood Park's iconic water tower displays the town's pride during the diamond jubilee in 1989. The tower was built as part of the water system modernization program in 1954. The 250,000-gallon tank was originally a silver/gray color, and it was first painted white in October 1963.

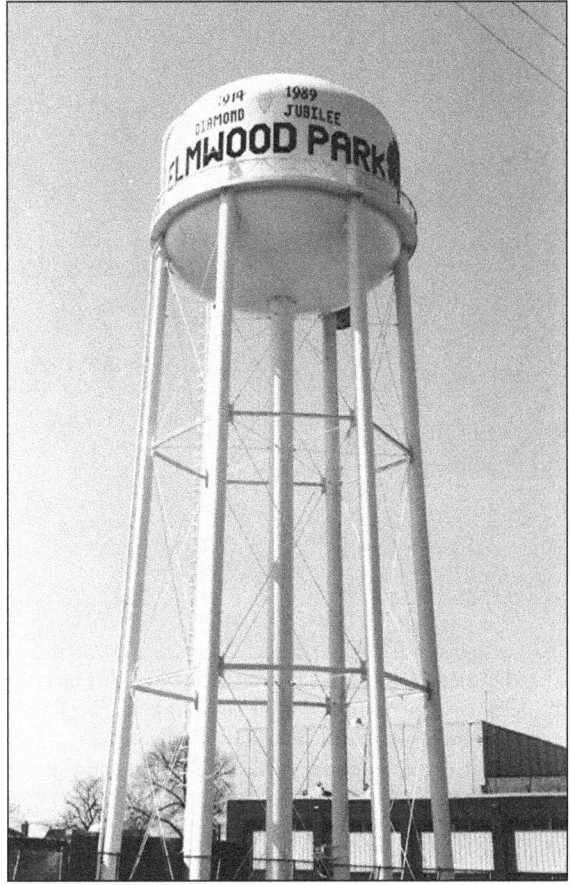

This type of locomotive pulled trains through Elmwood Park in the early 1980s. The Chicago, Milwaukee, St. Paul and Pacific Railroad, also known as the Milwaukee Road, was the train that made Elmwood Park famous. The railroad, in existence from 1847 to 1980, went bankrupt a couple of times before being purchased by Soo Line in 1986.

The defunct Goldblatts store at 2430 North Harlem Avenue (see page 56) was resurrected in the 1980s as Catherine Mall. The mall featured a number of businesses that catered to the large Italian population in the area. Gradually, the businesses either closed or relocated. The building was finally demolished in 2012. The vacant land is currently used as a parking lot.

Fire station No. 1 is seen here in July 2001. The facility, at 7 Conti Parkway, was constructed 12 years earlier, on the site of an old gas station and is one of several municipal structures designed by resident architect Charles E. "Gino" Petrungaro, including a public works building. The fire station was built using state funds, at no additional expense to the taxpayers of the village.

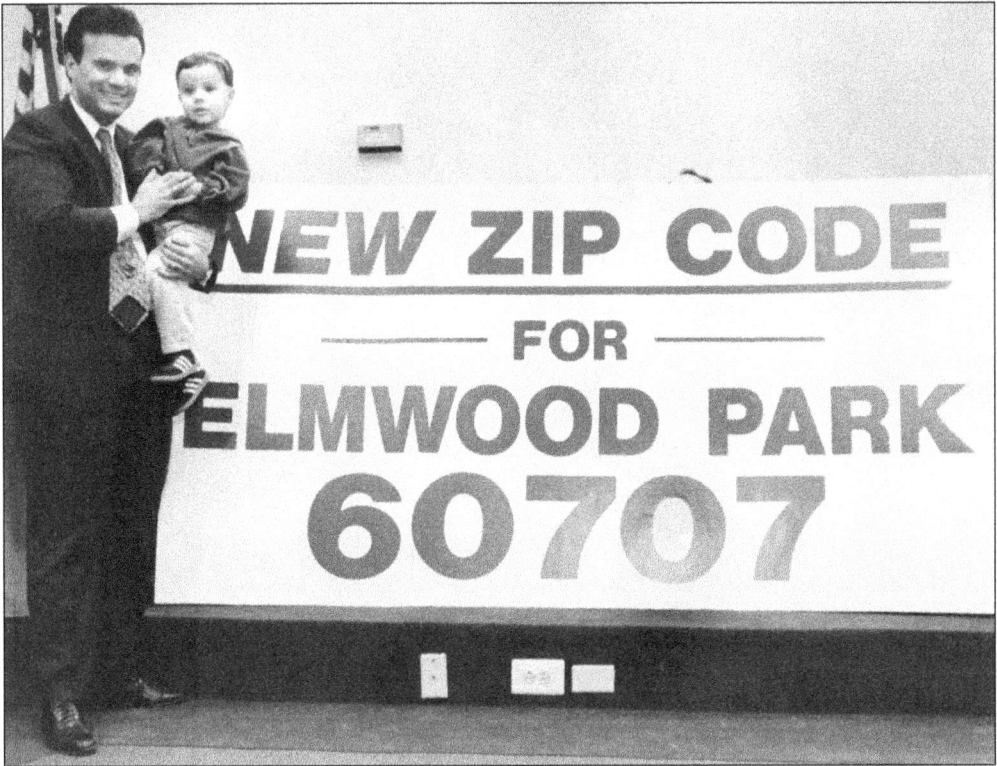

Village president Peter Silvestri and his son Christian welcome a new zip code for the village in 1997. After decades of sharing 60635 with parts of Chicago, the village requested the change to eliminate service delays and to allow residents to receive reduced insurance premiums for living in the suburbs. Ironically, the new zip code was also applied to several mail routes in the Galewood and Mount Clare sections of Chicago. (Courtesy of Village of Elmwood Park.)

Nearly 10 years passed between the time Central Park was dedicated on June 14, 1996, and when this photograph was taken in April 2006. In that time, the park has held summer concerts and the Taste of Elmwood Park, and has been the setting for many prom and wedding photographs. The park was created in 1995 when the village bought the land along Seventy-fifth Avenue from Marwood Avenue to Fullerton Avenue from R.O. Schultz. (Courtesy of Michael Warnock.)

The Kathie Torpe Playground is located at Fullerton and Seventy-sixth Avenues on land once owned by the library board. The park was named for a member of the board who died in late 1989. The village leased the land for $1 a year from the library board. In 2005, the park's name was shortened to Torpe Park to also honor Kathie's husband, Dick, who was once a village trustee and even served a short term as acting president.

On Saturday, June 7, 1997, the Family Aquatic Center opened for business. A photograph of this area 30 years earlier would have featured the Mills family French fountain. The V-shaped pool consists of dedicated swimming lanes and a zero-depth wading section. Other features include a slide, splash areas, concession stands, and plenty of room for sunbathers.

The public safety building at 7420 Fullerton Avenue was a blessing to both Fire Chief Kerry Hjellum and Police Chief Thomas Braglia when it was dedicated on August 16, 1997. It was built on the former site of fire station No. 2. The police department moved from the basement of the village hall into a modern and fully equipped facility. The current police force is authorized to have 36 full-time officers and 25 auxiliaries.

John Mills Park was a much-welcomed addition to the village's green space when it was dedicated on October 29, 1999. The park was created by closing off Seventy-sixth Avenue with a cul-de-sac and demolishing several buildings, including homes and a business. The park encompasses the former John Mills School playground, which had been an asphalt-covered, fenced-in enclosure.

On January 22, 2001, the day of ground breaking for the new library, some key players pose with an architectural rendering of the new building. Shown inside of the former library are, from left to right, state representative Skip Saviano, library board member Kevin Methling, contractor Ike Degan, library board president John Ferrentino, contractor Ray Rosato, architect Gino Petrungaro, village president Peter Silvestri, architect Joe Petrungaro, village manager John Jay Dalicandro, and village attorney Mike Durkin.

This photograph was taken on March 22, 2002, the day that the current library opened for business. Finishing touches such as landscaping had yet to be completed, but were finished by May 13, 2002, when the library was formally dedicated. The two-story structure was built on land that had been occupied by apartment buildings at Conti Parkway and the Avenue of Flags. It is the fifth and largest building to house the library.

Kids continue to be fascinated by the village's new war memorial, a 1942 three-inch, 75-millimeter artillery gun. The gun, which replaced the deteriorating World War II tank, was dedicated on Veterans Day 1999 and honors the villagers who gave the ultimate sacrifice for their country, like US Marine L.Cpl. Nickolas Daniels, who was killed in Afghanistan on November 5, 2011.

The residents of the 3000 block of Seventy-eighth Court revived the annual block party in 2007. A summertime tradition on many streets, block parties are often all-day affairs that include DJs, dancing, contests, and games. The event allows neighbors to interact with each other and, perhaps, to share some homemade wine or sausage. Some are elaborate affairs featuring themes, such as Hawaiian luaus, hoedowns, fiestas, or even toga parties. (Author's photograph.)

This photograph of sewer pipes at Eightieth Avenue and Sunset Drive in 2013 is reminiscent of the photograph on page 34. These pipes are part of the $20 million flood mitigation project begun in the spring of 2013. It is expected to take two years to complete. When finished, the system will carry excess floodwater to a reservoir in the Oak Park Country Club and. Eventually, the water will be pumped into the Des Plaines River. (Author's photograph.)

With President Silvestri's decision not to seek reelection, 2013 saw the first contested election in 20 years, as evidenced by this collection of campaign signs along Seventy-sixth Avenue. The election pitted Elmwood Park Voice Party candidate Joe Ponzio against longtime state representative for the 77th district and People's Choice Party candidate Angelo "Skip" Saviano, who won the election, becoming the 14th president of Elmwood Park. (Author's photograph.)

Seven

SAME PLACE, DIFFERENT TIME

The passing of years can have strange effects on one's memory. People will often think about a time or place and imagine it much differently than it actually was. Photographs capture the moment; they do not change. They may fade, become brittle perhaps, or even suffer water damage, but when viewed, they can bring back a flood of memories. It is hoped that the preceding chapters have brought back fond memories of places and people who may no longer be present, yet they will always remain a part of the community. For those who have not witnessed the changes firsthand, it can be difficult to imagine a location that is heard of or read about.

Elmwood Park has seen significant changes over the years. In the Circle, for example, buildings and facilities exist where once only trees, grass, and a beautiful French fountain once stood. Most of the Mills bungalows have been remodeled—be it the installation of dormers, a family-room addition, or even a complete second floor. The single-car Mills garages have in many cases been replaced with two-car garages.

Other changes are found among the business districts. Where factories and empty lots once stood, condominiums and townhomes have been built. Many familiar buildings fell to the wrecking ball. Some church congregations have grown and others have shrunk, and some have changed their names. A church became a park; a park became a civic center. The elm trees gave way to ash trees, only for these to be replaced themselves.

Yet other things stand the test of time, somehow adapting to the passing of years. They may look a bit different, but they function quite the same. In the course of 100 years, some things change and change again. This final chapter will attempt to reacquaint the reader with a place or location that he or she may not have thought about in many years, or give some perspective to those who are new to the village.

The above photograph, taken in 1933, looks southeast from the old bell tower of the municipal building. Seen here is Grand Avenue, which was once called Whiskey Point Road. The area was still rather rural at the time, and not much surrounded the train depot. Traffic was still held up by the ever-present trains that sever the village. Perhaps the most startling change is the Chicago skyline, which is present in the modern photograph below. The water tower is another feature that did not exist when the earlier photograph was taken. (Below, Bill Kucera photograph.)

By 1947, the intersection of Harlem and North Avenues was already a destination of sorts, with Hayes Restaurant and the Sky Club. The corner is just one of the gateways into Elmwood Park. The intersection divides four communities: Elmwood Park on the northwest; Chicago on the northeast; Oak Park on the southeast; and River Forest on the southwest. Sears and Walgreens have anchored two of those corners for quite some time. In 1927, only two businesses existed along North Avenue from Harlem to Thatcher Avenues—Hayes Restaurant and a real estate office. (Below, author's photograph.)

The views in these two photographs face north on Seventy-fifth Avenue. In the above photograph, taken in 1959, the crossing actually consists of four sets of tracks. Today's drivers can be thankful that at least one set has been removed. Just to the right of the photographer in 1959 would have been the R.O. Schulz factory site. It has since been leveled and replaced by the Grand Crossing townhomes. On the left, where once a few homes stood, Central Park now exists (see page 111). This crossing has seen many accidents over the years. For a time, there were no gates, only lights to warn motorists of approaching trains. (Below, author's photograph.)

Marsch's restaurant stood on the corner of North and Thatcher Avenues in 1960. Since the days of the Thatcher Inn, the corner has often been a destination for those seeking inexpensive meals as they traveled along North Avenue. The strip of North Avenue from Thatcher Avenue to First Avenue was popular with hot-rodders who often raced their cars and ended up at Marsch's or Russell's. In 1961, Marsch's owner, Harry Birtman, wanted to build a 42-unit motel on the site, which the village fought. Birtman passed away in 1965 and, eventually, his building gave way to the mixed-use structure that stands on the corner today. (Below, author's photograph.)

The Elmwood Park Presbyterian Church, seen above in 1950, was organized in 1943. In recent years, the church, located at 7600 West Armitage Avenue, suffered from a declining congregation. The building was demolished in 2012 and has been replaced by Centennial Park, which has added some much-needed open space to the south side of the village. The new park, which is less than an acre in size, offers a workout area, raised flower beds, and a bocce court. The park was officially dedicated on May 3, 2013. (Below, author's photograph.)

The above photograph was taken looking west down Barry Avenue from Seventy-eighth Avenue in 1939. The large open field was an area extending from Seventy-sixth Court, west to Eightieth Avenue, and from Barry Avenue on the north to Wellington Avenue. This was the last section of Westwood to be developed, most likely because Mills & Sons declared bankruptcy in 1932. While the rest of the area is composed of Mills bungalows, this area was completed with built-to-order homes of different styles. Buick and Guild constructed about 125 of the 196 homes. The houses along Metropole Street were built by John S. Clark & Son, and several more were erected by Mills & Sons, which was back in business by 1939. (Below, author's photograph.)

The above photograph shows the corner of Grand and Harlem Avenues in 1972. The Ablin's building was the home of the first tavern in town. The corner is the epicenter of the Elmwood Park–Mont Clare shopping area and once featured Steinberg Baum, a general merchandise retailer, as well as Goldblatts, which was just up the street on Harlem Avenue. The below photograph shows the same scene in 2013. A Circuit City store had been built on the northwest corner and sat empty after it closed. The building was purchased, extensively rehabbed, and opened as the new flagship store for the Angelo Caputo's Fresh Markets grocery chain on February 16, 2010. On May 3, 2013, the new gateway fountain was built to welcome visitors into the village. (Below, author's photograph.)

The unknown canine guardian of the alleyways in the above photograph, taken in the 1930s, would still probably recognize his old haunts today. Although many of the garages seen in this photograph have been replaced by two- or two-and-a-half-car garages, many of the original Mills one-car garages remain. One thing new to Fido would be the surface of the alley. As part of the ongoing initiative to alleviate flooding in the area, four alleys were made "green" in 2012. With funding from an Environmental Protection Agency grant, the unique alleys were reconstructed to channel water to the center section, composed of bricks and crushed stone. This allows the water to soak in rather than run off into the storm drains. The alley shown here is on Seventy-eighth Avenue between Elmgrove and Sunset Drives. (Below, author's photograph.)

The Elmwood Park station on the Milwaukee Road line was in its prime in 1935, when the above photograph was taken. In the background is Hal Chapman's Tavern, which was located at 2431 North Seventy-fifth Court, the site of which is now a part of Central Park. The 1927 station fell into disrepair and was demolished in 1977. It was replaced by small concrete shelters, which have also been replaced. In 2006, a new Metra station was dedicated. The structure offers much more shelter to travelers. In 2005, it was calculated that 82 trains pass each day—52 passenger and 30 freight trains. (Below, author's photograph.)

The municipal building and the structure at 12 Conti Parkway are two local landmarks. The mixed-use building, which began as the Westwood Bank, is now home to the Sweet & Simple Bakery and Caroline's. Village president John Beck's body lay in state at the municipal building when the village lost its young leader, who died suddenly at the age of 33 on July 20, 1929. The building, erected during Beck's presidency, has seen many changes over the years, including renovations in 1984 designed to make it handicapped-accessible—prior to the Americans with Disabilities Act of 1990. The eastern wing of the building, which once housed the fire department, became a community center. It was named the Josette LaFrambois Center in 1999. The police department and the building department were housed in the western wing. The Peace Monument (below) was installed in 1980. (Below, author's photograph.)

Visit us at
arcadiapublishing.com